COLOSTRUM

NATURE'S
HEALING
Miracle

D0777952

Donald R. Henderson, MD, MPH
Deborah Mitchell

Foreword By Kaye Wyatt

Published by CNR Publications

Colostrum - Nature's Healing Miracle is intended solely for informational and educational purposes, and not as medical advice. Please consult a medical or health professional if you have questions about your health.

COLOSTRUM - NATURE'S HEALING MIRACLE

Printed in the United States of America

Published by
CNR Publications
PO Box 4387
Sedona, AZ 86340

CNR Publications is a subsidiary of CNR, Inc.
a non-profit, independent research organization.

Table of Contents

FOREWARD
by Kaye Wyatt

Five years ago, Kaye Wyatt co-authored the book, Colostrum, Life's First Food, that brought colostrum to the public's awareness. For the book, she and her husband Doug gathered and compiled the extensive medical studies on colostrum that they found buried on the back shelves of the medical library (more medical research than on all other natural substances combined). Medical research on a substance usually becomes available to the consumer only after the substance is approved as a drug.

Kaye's story includes her experience of healing from her first book and an update on how colostrum has helped her over the last five years. Today, Kaye and her husband Doug travel all over the world speaking to health practitioners and the general public about the amazing substance that saved Kaye's life.

This evening, Mother Nature was about to give one of her finest performances. As she calmed the breeze, she gave all of summer's wondrous smells, sounds and sights center stage – the fragrance of catalpa blossoms, the laughter of ducks, and one of Salt Lake City's spectacular sunsets. Sitting next to my husband on our deck that overlooks the valley, I realized that even after all these years, he still had the power to make my heart skip a beat. The peace and euphoria became intoxicating as we waited for the show to begin. The sun had slipped behind the clouds in its reach for the western mountains. Pirate ships, illuminated in gold, took form in the clouds as the slanting rays went into hiding. Their massive sails looked innocent in shades of pink but suddenly graduated to fiery red against the turquoise sea. Pirate ships – pirates – were they coming for me? Quickly, I closed my eyes, willing these menacing images to disappear. In their place, I pictured the special people who make my life so wonderful – a mother I adore, a supportive brother, three almost perfect children and nine perfect grandchildren.

It seems that my husband Doug and I have always had the ability to know what the other was thinking at any given moment, so it was no surprise that when my tears came, I saw them mirrored in my husband. Several weeks earlier, I was

diagnosed with Legionnaire's Disease. (I can't imagine how I contracted it.) The doctors flooded my body with the most powerful antibiotics available. I don't remember ever being that sick. I believed that the antibiotics had cured this disease but the doctors weren't so confident. They told me that if I should start feeling sick again, they might not be able to help me. I do believe that our expectations create our reality and so I've made an effort to be optimistic despite my health challenges. I was even criticized once for living in a fantasy, happy-ever-after world instead of the real world.

Well, I *was* getting sick again. I had to tell my husband, the man who had chosen to walk this difficult path with me for all these years and who loved me so much that he was always there cheering me on, that things didn't look very good. My optimism was crumbling – I was so tired of fighting – I felt for the first time that there might not be a "happy ever after" for us.

My entrance into this world set the precedent for how I would approach every problem in my life – hit it head on, expect everything to work out and get it behind you. My mother barely made it to the hospital in time. My parents were thrilled that they had a boy first and that now they had a little girl. Their elation changed to fear after they brought me home from the hospital. My breathing became erratic and labored and they realized that I was in serious trouble. There was no sleep for my mother as she lay by my side, clutching my hand. It took only one time for me to stop breathing altogether and turn blue to make them insist on an answer from the doctor. I think that I was born during the dark ages of medicine because treatment for respiratory distress at that time consisted of extensive radiation of the thymus gland. I can't imagine that they didn't know that the thymus gland is the master control of the immune system.

This procedure virtually destroyed my immune system, and my life from that point forward became a constant battle of life-threatening infections and allergies. The first allergy my parents noticed was to cow's milk. I did okay on goat's milk but it could only be purchased from farmers who lived a great distance from our house. To get enough goat's milk to last a couple of days, my father had to get up at the crack of dawn and find it before everyone else did. Despite all my parents' efforts to keep me away from known allergens, I was continually struggling with asthma, hives and eczema. I can vividly recall vacations at an age that I should have been too young to

Colostrum *Nature's Healing Miracle*

remember because of our little side trips to get medical help for my asthma. When I was older, they were able to control the severity of my asthma attacks with drugs and cortisone shots. This set the stage for the fight of my life – my fight for survival – equipped only with a radiation-weakened immune system and drugs that proved to be deadly boomerangs.

After the birth of my third child, I was teaching at the junior high school and constantly battling bacterial and viral infections. Between the germs that my children brought home and the germs that I picked up at school, I remember taking an antibiotic almost every month for fifteen years. I was so busy teaching and raising three children that my doctor would tell me to skip coming in to his office to be checked, and he would just phone in a prescription. The thought never entered my mind that taking this many antibiotics could possibly hurt me.

When I was twenty-five, I had a partial hysterectomy and should have recovered fully within a month's time. Three weeks after the hysterectomy, I was still in the hospital with infection and recurring hemorrhaging. I came home looking like a skeleton and it took months, with my mother's help, to get me back on my feet. A couple of years after that, I had all four wisdom teeth removed in two sessions. I remember my dentist reassuring me that only a very small percentage of people experience a dry socket after extraction. Both teeth removed in the first session left dry sockets that took months to heal. I remember the pain being unbearable. He assured me that it couldn't happen again. With me, it could and it did.

About ten years ago, I had finally reached the point where I was unable to work because of constant dental surgeries and associated infections, which called for more antibiotics. Root canal surgeries could not be done the traditional way. The dentist had to go through the gums because my roots had calcified. He said that he thought this was caused from an allergy to the metals that were used or prior trauma to the teeth from extensive work.

It was right after that, that as much as I needed to work and as much as I wanted to work, I couldn't. I would last only a couple of hours each morning before my temperature would soar and I would collapse in bed. I was so weak that something as simple as washing and drying my hair was a major accomplishment. It's amazing to me how everything in the body goes downhill when the immune system is not working. My physical appearance was very upsetting, so much so that I avoided letting anyone take my picture, and it actually hurt to look at myself in the mirror. I bought scar cover-up to hide the fever blisters that constantly covered the lower portion of my face. I used wigs, nail polish, loose clothing and a smile to camouflage my unhealthy appearance. The smile was the most difficult because of all the problems I was having that couldn't be camouflaged – high blood pressure, increasingly irregular heart palpitations, reactive hypoglycemic symptoms (even though my diet was closely monitored), serious digestive problems, headaches, sinus congestion, dizziness and buzzing in the ears, muscle soreness and joint pain that kept me awake at night, mental confusion, panic attacks, fatigue beyond description, crying spells, and severe and sometimes almost unbearable depression.

At that point, life was not only difficult for me but for my husband as well. He could never count on me for anything – a vacation, a day's adventure, or even an evening out. Eventually, I would get so angry with myself and force myself to go out for a day or an evening with my husband. Within a very short time, my rising fever would forbid any enjoyment for me with demanding thoughts of wanting to be home in bed. I honestly don't know if I would have had his patience if our roles had been reversed.

During those years, Doug and I investigated everything that traditional and alternative medicine had to offer. Anyone who has experienced this unsuccessfully as we did, knows the strain it can put on the emotions and pocketbook. Today, when someone tells me about a wonderful new substance or treatment, I am not interested in the clever advertising; I want to see the medical research on the product.

We did find a few things that supported us during those years. I took several correspondence classes through the university on nutrition, and Doug purchased several health-related cookbooks (his hobby is cooking). Every week, Doug visited the library and ended up bringing home stacks of books. We found the mind-body connection to be the most promising.

As the setting sun presented its grand finale before leaving the stage, with tears in place of words, Doug took my hand and asked me not to give up hope.

I've always asked Doug not to let anyone know how sick I was, especially family members that might worry. The next morning, at a business meeting, Doug was introduced to a doctor from Belgium who was involved with natural healing supplements. Doug later told me that he couldn't stop himself from talking nonstop to the doctor about the problem we were facing. The doctor asked Doug if we had used colostrum and encouraged him to purchase a jar of powdered colostrum from him for $160. Doug was so excited when he brought it home, telling me all about the immune and growth factors that could boost my immune system. I told him that the last thing I needed right now were growth factors to make my feet grow bigger (that doesn't happen, of course). I realized how vulnerable Doug was because of our situation but I couldn't believe he had fallen for another miracle cure, with no research and only a naturopathic doctor's testimony to back it.

It was the next day that I fell and seriously injured my knee. I hemorrhaged into the kneecap which became the size of a grapefruit. We immediately went to the emergency room where they put my leg in a Velcro cast. They told me to stay off my feet and keep my leg elevated for a couple of weeks. When I got home, I was still so sick and in so much pain from my injury that I told Doug, "Okay, I'll take your stupid medicine." I firmly believed that it would be a disappointment like everything else I had tried. I think the real reason I took it was because I wanted Doug to finally accept the reality that there would be no miracle cure for me. I took a heaping tablespoonful of the colostrum with some water. I couldn't sleep with the cast on, so Doug helped me take it off.

The next morning, Doug was the first one up and was reading the newspaper when I came in. I started pouring myself some juice when he looked at me in a funny way and kept repeating my name. It took a moment before I realized that I was standing, pain free, on a leg that I couldn't put any weight on the evening before. I looked down at my knee that showed no indication that anything had ever happened to it, except for a faint bruise on the side of the kneecap.

This was the beginning of a new life for me. It was a couple of days later that I broke my temperature for the last time! So many changes occurred in my body which, I discovered later, were attributable to the colostrum.

During this time, I had the honor of working with Ormond McGill, an outstanding hypnotherapist known throughout the world. I feel that this work made it possible for me to survive until I found colostrum.

Two years prior to this time, my doctor tested me for sero-

tonin (neurotransmitter) uptake because I was having episodes of severe depression. He told me that my test results were the worst he had ever seen. He said he was reluctant to even let me leave his office because people in my condition were known, in a split second, to do something drastic to end their lives, like drive off a cliff. I didn't realize I was that bad. The antidepressants that the doctor put me on were unsuccessful, causing frightening side-effects.

Colostrum has helped me so much with my depression. As I understand it, colostrum helps balance production of the "feel-good" neurotransmitter chemicals, serotonin and dopamine. It also keeps the blood-sugar levels regulated throughout the day, which helps enhance both mental clarity and energy levels. I have purposely not taken colostrum for a couple of days to see if I would notice a difference. I found that my thinking isn't as clear, my energy and motivation are low, and according to one of my friends, I'm not my happy self. She asked me, "You have stopped taking your colostrum, haven't you?" This is probably the biggest reason why most people who have used colostrum never want to be without it again.

I had another pleasant surprise. The naturopathic doctor who introduced us to colostrum said that it might help my gingivitis. My dentist felt that I might have to consider gum surgery because it was so advanced (very sensitive teeth and sore and bleeding gums). I faithfully packed my gums with powdered colostrum every evening for a couple of weeks while I watched TV. That's all it took. On my next visit, my dentist couldn't believe that I showed no signs of gingivitis. He is now recom-mending colostrum to all his patients.

Almost a year after I started taking colostrum, I went to visit my daughter in a small town in Wyoming. I was greeted with hugs and kisses by all of her husband's family (they accounted for a good portion of the town's population). I was told a year earlier that if I got pneumonia again, I couldn't count on antibi-otics to help. Within days, I started getting a little nervous when everyone was complaining of colds and raw sore throats, and some were admitted to the hospital with bacterial pneumonia. I had done everything I could in the first two days of my visit to run down my immune system. My daughter and I ate dough-nuts for breakfast, went swimming in the outdoor hot-springs pool in freezing temperatures, and ate more of all those good things that we knew we shouldn't eat. This would certainly be the ultimate test for colostrum. My daughter and I got the snif-

Colostrum *Nature's Healing Miracle*

fles for about an hour one morning and that was it (she also takes colostrum). My immune system won then and still keeps winning. I haven't had a cold or the flu since I started taking colostrum. Also, I have been able to go without allergy shots or inhalants for asthma and have not experienced any problems.

While in Wyoming, I received an unexpected compliment when I went swimming with my daughter at the hot springs. I forgot my bathing suit and had to borrow one from her (it would have to be a bikini). The cute young lifeguard at the pool was actually flirting with me. He asked my daughter if I was her sister. I felt like a butterfly emerging from its cocoon. It wasn't very long ago that it took all the courage that I had just to go out in public. For more than ten years, I was unable to do any physical activity. I had gained weight, especially around my waist, and my muscles had atrophied and been replaced by fat and cellulite. My grandchildren's comments spoke the unhappy truth. "Grandma, what's all that fat stuff hanging over your knees," they would ask. Their eyes would always scan my arms and hands which were covered with age spots, rashes and raised veins from poor circulation.. One of my youngest grand-daughters had tears in her eyes as she said, "Oh, Grandma, you have too many boo-boos."

I have definitely noticed some changes in my physical body in the first year of using colostrum. The most dramatic change I have noticed is with my muscle tone. After years in bed, it was almost nonexistent. My muscles are now toned, with no trace of cellulite. My daughter, who is a physical trainer, recently checked my body fat. She explained that an 18-to-27 body-fat percentage is the ideal for someone in their twenties. My body fat was 24 percent! I'm now able to wear the same size jeans that I wore in my early twenties. My cholesterol and blood pressure are better than perfect. My hair is finally healthy, shiny and all the same length, which was impossible before with severe breakage and loss. I noticed that my toenails were growing in pink, flat and healthy. Before colostrum, the doctor was considering removing them because of an advanced fun-gus, a result of years of antibiotic use.

I don't know if it is the radiance of health and feeling on top of the world or the outward physical changes, but everyone who has taken colostrum for at least a couple of months looks shockingly younger. Throughout history, we've been searching for the fountain of youth – I think the search is over!

In my excitement, I wanted everyone in the world to experi-

Colostrum *Nature's Healing Miracle*

ence the healing that I had experienced with colostrum. I found that a few people whom I talked to would go on and on about how sick they were, but the minute I mentioned that I might have something that could help them, they would recoil and abruptly end the conversation. This was very unsettling until I remembered something I've known for a long time – there are a lot of people who really want to be sick. Sickness has always contained an element of control and escapism.

As a child, we were coddled by our mothers whenever we ran a fever, and seriously ill adults are still given intensive care. I've witnessed people who hold the belief that suffering is meaningful and inevitable, even a grace. These emotions, beliefs and expectations that are connected to illness are usually established in early childhood. They are so deeply embedded in the subconscious mind that they probably won't be changed or even recognized in this lifetime.

For example, one lady, who suffers from a crippling disease that the doctors have not been able to put a name to, has her husband's complete, undivided attention. Most of their time is spent traveling to exotic places around the world, seeking a cure. I was distressed to hear how sick she was, so I gave her some research information and free samples of colostrum. She returned the samples a week later explaining that this wasn't the right time for her to start the colostrum. She told me that she was under a lot of stress with the holidays coming up and felt that she might be coming down with the flu. She said that she really thought it would be best to wait until she felt better before she started taking the colostrum.

A word of warning: If you take colostrum, you might never get sympathy again. Doug went out of town on business for a couple of days. I tripped on a chair leg and either broke or seriously sprained my big toe. It swelled and turned purple clear up to my ankle. My neighbor, a nurse, looked at my foot and said that I probably wouldn't be able to wear a shoe for at least a month. How was I going to pick up my husband in two days at the airport? I increased my intake of colostrum, and, miraculously, I walked the length of the airport to meet his plane. There was no pain, no swelling, no discoloration – and no sympathy!

I have talked with so many people about how colostrum has dramatically changed their lives. One of my favorite stories is from a lady who has suffered with crippling arthritis for years. Colostrum has made it possible for her to walk again and resume the hobbies she loves, without pain. Several months ago, her veterinarian recommended that she put the family dog to sleep because he was showing signs of heart failure. He was listless, barely eating, and his body was bloating. She and her grown children were distraught. In desperation, she sprinkled colostrum in what little food he would eat. Within days, he had his appetite back, his bloating had disappeared, and he was playfully acting like a puppy. She recently shared with us that his coat is shiny again, he is so active, and that he seems to have forgotten his age. But most important, she said, "He's always smiling." Her children were so shocked at the changes in the dog that they have all started taking colostrum.

Two stories of healing that happened to people close to me show how you can sometimes tell exactly where colostrum is doing its work in the body – it is the location where you may experience increased sensitivity or discomfort for a short time. My brother recently had surgery on his leg. I told him to take lots of colostrum so it would heal quicker. He told me that it made his leg hurt more and was also causing pain in his shoulder where he had had surgery six months ago. I told him that this was good news and that he should definitely take more colostrum. He didn't understand why I said this until I told him about what happened to Doug's knee shortly after he started taking colostrum.

Doug received a donor tendon in his knee after an accident on the trampoline with our grandchildren. The doctors told him that he would not be able to bend his knee a full 90 degrees and to expect periodic pain. He started on the colostrum and every day the pain got worse. Two weeks later, he could barely walk because of the pain, and he said that he thought he should stop taking the colostrum. It was that night that he woke me up at 3:00 AM to show me that he could bend his leg more than 90 degrees. He has not experienced any pain with his knee whatsoever since then. To watch him on the stair machine, you would never believe he had ever had a problem.

Colostrum works. It really works! Remember, however, that each one of us is unique in regard to age, weight, progression of illness, and lifestyle. We each require varying amounts of colostrum because it is a food, not a drug, and its effects cannot be quantified. Research shows that it has no drug interactions and it is completely safe at any level, with no side effects. I have found that my body needs more colostrum than that of most people. You need to work with your own body and let it tell you what it needs. But most of all, please be patient. Although colostrum begins its healing and tissue repair immediately, it may have some work to do.

The only problem I see with colostrum is that it may sound too good to be true. It scares me to think how close I came to not using it! I sometimes wonder how and why colostrum did come to me. I am probably one of the world's biggest skeptics – I have to prove everything to myself – not just once, but with every test imaginable. Maybe someone knew that if colostrum passed all *my* stringent tests, I would share it with the world.

KAYE'S STORY CONTINUED (FIVE YEARS LATER)

I would like to share four stories about unexpected healing with colostrum that have happened to me over the last five years. These experiences have left me in awe of this miraculous healing substance. I feel that Dr. Donald Henderson summed it up best when he said, "Kaye, after reviewing the research and what I have experienced with my patients, I don't think that you and Doug have any idea of what colostrum can do." I told him that after the miracles that have happened in my life, I felt I might have some idea. He said, "No, Kaye, you have no idea!"

HEALING AT THE CELLULAR LEVEL

Almost twenty years ago, I had a water-skiing accident in which a ski penetrated my left temple. I was in the hospital for over a month and was told that I had irreversible nerve damage which affected my vision and speech. My eyes focused at different levels, making it almost impossible to read or work at the computer without getting severe headaches, and I couldn't speak without stuttering. Apparently, however, the word 'irreversible' doesn't mean much when you're taking colostrum. I no longer have any problems with my vision or speech. I have even taken the step of speaking about colostrum in front of groups of people – something that would have been unthinkable earlier.

STRENGTHENING THE IMMUNE SYSTEM

Doug and I had the opportunity to take the vacation of a lifetime. First, we spent ten days exploring all of South Island and North Island in New Zealand, and then we spent another ten days at a beautiful, remote resort in Fiji. The highlight for me in

Colostrum *Nature's Healing Miracle*

New Zealand was the opportunity to tour the farms and plants where the colostrum is processed. I wanted to understand why only New Zealand Dairy Group's colostrum worked for me. As the Kiwis would say, "I was blown away!" Everything was so state-of-the-art and pristine. We were even asked to don white coats, shoe covers and headgear prior to entering their administrative offices. I now understand why New Zealand Dairy Group has the highest quality rating in the world for its dairy products.

Our first week in Fiji was magic – the friendly natives, the romantic evenings and the pink coral reef that beckoned us to explore its secrets. On one of our dives my mask came loose and I breathed in instead of breathing out. The pressure forced water and a rare bacteria into the mastoids (the large, bony cavity that is positioned behind the ear). Mastoid infections are nasty because bacteria thrive on bone tissue, and the blood supply to this area can be so limited that neither antibiotics nor colostrum is able to reach it. I had to cut my colostrum dose in half because we had given away so many bottles during the trip. It would have taken forever to have more colostrum shipped to us. The infection that started in the mastoid spread to the inner ear.

We moved to another resort so we could be near a doctor. The doctor put me on antibiotics and told me that I wouldn't be able to fly home with Doug or even fly home at all until the infection was gone and I could clear my ears. It was so scary to be all alone half way around the world and not know when I would be able to go home. Every day for a week I checked in with the doctor who told me, "Not today." I spent that whole week renting Walt Disney videos (that is all they had) and ordering room service. I couldn't believe how emotional I was when the doctor told me that I could go home, and again when the airplane landed in Los Angeles. I couldn't stop the tears that were streaming down my face. I think that I had a little fear, given my history, that I might never see home again.

For the next ten months, I experienced only a slight pain behind the ear and then the infection spread once again, to the ear canal. An ear, nose and throat specialist at home gave the same diagnosis as the doctor in Fiji – a simple ear infection. He treated me with numerous antibiotics and put a tube in my left ear. Every day for weeks, my ear drained more than it did the day before and the pain behind my ear increased.

We had just met Dr. Donald Henderson. Doug mentioned

the problems that I was having with my ear. He couldn't believe that my doctor hadn't ordered an MRI. He referred me to another specialist and arranged an immediate MRI to be scheduled. I can imagine what our little hospital thought when the chief of staff of Los Angeles' biggest hospital called and placed the order. I know that Dr. Henderson saved my life with his caring and quick action. The MRI showed exactly what he expected it might – the left mastoid was filled with infection and there was some infection in the right mastoid. Left untreated, the infection could spread to the brain, bringing coma and possibly death.

The specialist explained that the only way to reach and stop this infection, short of surgery, was to get on the big guns (massive steroids to break down the walls of the veins leading to the mastoid, and IV-drip antibiotics twice a day for two weeks). The veins throughout my entire body became so damaged that after a week and a half, IV fluid leaked from the veins in my arms. This regimen is beyond a nightmare with its toll on the body and the emotions. The home healthcare nurse told me that most people can usually only follow this regimen for a week and then have to quit. I knew that if I didn't make it, I would be looking at surgery. I did make it, however, and I know it was because the colostrum was protecting my body. I experienced none of the health problems that usually follow this type of assault on the body.

HEALING THE DIGESTIVE TRACT

My husband and I have read a lot of books recently about food allergies. We also have a lot of friends and family members who have had comprehensive tests to find the foods that they should avoid because of an allergy. Some people have told us that their list of foods to avoid goes on and on. It is only natural that my husband would take the next step and schedule the two of us for a full, comprehensive food-allergy test.

I was stalling. I knew that the foods I loved and would sometimes eat, like breads and chocolate, would be at the top of my list. Ever since I was a new baby, I have had an allergic reaction to so many foods. I have always been careful about what I eat, and I just didn't want the doctor to tell me that I could never cheat. We went ahead with the test and after a week, I got so antsy that I called the nurse to see when the report would be back. She told me that she had just received my report and that

all the nurses in the office were talking about me. I thought, "Oh great – it's worse than I thought." She then told me that I was the first person whose test had come back with NO FOOD ALLERGIES!

After reading some new research reports on the critical importance of bowel health (something that we won't even talk about to ourselves), I realized how seriously ill I was before colostrum. I feel that this is the area where people using colostrum will notice a difference immediately.

Food allergies can be evidence of bowel permeability. Most adults in this country have what is termed Leaky Gut Syndrome. There are holes in the bowel lining that substances (pathogens, toxins, and even food particles) can cross and find their way into the blood. When these partially digested food particles are absorbed into the bloodstream, the body attacks them as a foreign antigen, or invader, creating an allergic reaction.

I now have a medical test confirming the extent to which colostrum can heal the digestive tract. The doctor was absolutely shocked at my report and said that he was going to get more serious about taking his colostrum.

Note: You may find that as colostrum heals the digestive tract, drugs and supplements that you take every day may finally be more fully utilized by the body, creating a more pronounced effect.

HORMONAL BALANCE

I'm certain that every woman in our country over the age of 40 can relate to the confusion I have experienced concerning whether or not to take hormone replacement therapy. I began taking estrogen (Premarin) at age 26 after my partial hysterectomy. My doctor said I would need it for the rest of my life to ward off osteoporosis, which does run in my family. For twenty years, I experienced all the nasty symptoms of too much estrogen because my ovaries were still producing it. I started my menopause early, at about age 45. It was about this time that all the conflicting information came out about hormone replacement therapy. I tried everything that traditional and alternative medicine had to offer, from Estradiol and natural progesterone cream to soy and natural progesterone cream, and on and on. Those years were miserable trying to just stay afloat and I reached the point where I refused to take anything.

Soon after that, I started taking colostrum. I should have guessed that this miraculous substance that brings the body back in harmony was also accomplishing this with my female hormones. All the clues were there. My figure is actually better than it was at age sixteen – tight muscles, small waist, and curves where they should be. I no longer experience hormonal mood swings. I have none of the changes that occur after menopause.

My doctor recently gave me a lecture on why I should take estrogen. I asked him if I could have a blood test to measure my estrogen level because I didn't see how I could feel any better than I did. My doctor was shocked (again!) when the test came back – my estrogen level was the same as that of a young girl at the beginning of her cycle – not enough to start her cycle but just the perfect level for a woman of my age to live life to its fullest!

IN CONCLUSION

I want to thank all the people who have recently put so much of their time and effort into gathering information, researching, and writing to help bring colostrum to the public's awareness. I especially want to thank Donald Henderson, MD, for stepping up and caring enough to write and speak about this remarkable rediscovery.

Last, but most important, I want to thank those of you who are sharing information and research on colostrum with your doctors and the people you love. There are so many children and adults who are suffering from poor health who have given up hope. You are the ones who are taking us one step closer to reaching these people and giving them hope for a new life.

Colostrum *Nature's Healing Miracle*

INTRODUCTION

The biggest threat to our health today is the growing number of disease-causing organisms which are partially or completely resistant to an alarming number of antibiotics. This is a serious worldwide problem that has the potential to affect the health and well-being of every man, woman, and child. Another threat is the constant assault on the body by disease-promoting substances, such as cigarette smoke, gasoline fumes, toxins in the water, pesticides in and on food, and exposure to radiation. These environmental poisons are dangerous to everyone, but especially to the very young, the elderly, and anyone whose immune system is in a weakened state, such as those with AIDS, cancer, candida, lupus, respiratory disease, and dozens of other medical conditions.

As a physician who specializes in gastroenterology, I am greatly concerned about the increasing number of antibiotics that are becoming ineffective, particularly as we discover more and more diseases that are caused by infectious agents. New research shows that many diseases such as heart disease, gastric cancer, and peptic ulcer, that were previously thought to be caused by other factors, may well be caused by infectious agents. In effect, we are losing the battle: there are more and more diseases to fight with a declining arsenal of ammunition with which to battle them effectively, until now.

When I first heard about colostrum, I was skeptical. Researchers and advocates of the supplement claimed it was a powerful, all-natural antibiotic, effective against a great number of organisms towards which conventional antibiotics are losing their effectiveness. They said it could protect the body against the constant barrage of disease-promoting substances in the environment. I decided to investigate these claims for myself. And what I found was exciting and promising. I began recommending colostrum to many of my patients—for colitis, gastritis, Crohn's disease, and other gastrointestinal disorders. And it worked. What's more, both research and anecdotal stories show that colostrum is effective in treating a wide range of conditions – not just these gastrointestinal problems—conditions such as rheumatoid arthritis, and allergies.

This book shares my excitement with you. It is the story of colostrum—what it is, its many healing components, and its effectiveness in combating many health problems. Learn what I discovered about colostrum and how it can significantly improve your health—today and for the rest of your life.

DID YOU KNOW THAT...

- **Children who are breast-fed have higher IQs and less neurological dysfunctions than children who are not breast-fed.**

- **Infants who are breast-fed are one-fifth to one-third less likely to die of sudden infant death syndrome.**

- **Lactating protects women against osteoporosis, while not breastfeeding is a risk factor for its development.**

- **Formula-fed infants are 10 to 15 times more likely to become hospitalized when ill than breast-fed infants.**

Every moment of every day you are exposed to substances that have the ability to make you sick—whether it be an innocuous condition such as the common cold or nausea, or an insidious disease such as cancer or heart disease. The body makes every attempt to fight, destroy, and otherwise deal with disease-causing invaders. But it is a difficult task, and a job that is increasingly hard for the body to continue to do efficiently and effectively, especially as you get older and your body's immune system becomes overburdened from the continuous battle to protect your health. You need help to prevent illness and maintain optimal wellness. That help is available in a substance that is natural, safe, and effective. It's a substance that is as basic as motherhood and life itself. That help is called colostrum, and the story begins at the beginning of life.

The Miracle of Birth

It is time.

She lies on a carpet of green, her swollen stomach heavy against the dew-flecked grass. Her legs are stretched out before her, wet from the water bag that burst just moments ago. The contractions have been coming in waves for nearly an hour, but they are quickening now, with an urgency. She strains and braces herself against the earth. Now, the nine months of waiting are nearly over. From the birth canal, the feet appear first. There is another strong contraction, followed by the hint of a nose, and then the baby comes quickly—the ears, the head, and the rest of the body in a final, quivering thrust.

The baby slides to the ground, glistening in the moonlight. It's a girl, a tangle of legs and mucus, helpless and vulnerable. Her mother is tired, but not so much that she neglects her duty or fails to fulfill what she and her ancestors have always done after bringing a new life into the world. She reaches over to her offspring and cleans her, licking the mucus from her nostrils and prompting the flow of blood and oxygen through her body.

She waits, truly exhausted now, for the miracle is not yet over. A new life has been introduced to the world; now she must help sustain it. The frail, gangly calf struggles to reach its mother's underbelly, nuzzles up to its mother's teat, and takes its first meal—its gift of life. There will be no life for the calf if it doesn't get the gift of colostrum. Within minutes, the once frail calf has the energy to stand with the herd and, if need be, make a valiant attempt to escape danger — colostrum is that powerful.

Breastfeeding and Colostrum

Research shows that newborn calves need colostrum within the first 24 hours of life — not only to build their immune systems but also to give them the essential support for optimal metabolic functioning. A delay of colostrum for as little as one day can be a death sentence for these young creatures.[1]

This special gift of colostrum from mother to child is not unique among cows. All female mammals are designed to breastfeed their offspring. Breastfeeding is a natural, critical function in the mammalian world. Most human infants are not so different from calves or piglets or puppies. When newborn mammals first enter the world, they are dependent on their mother to give them their "second start" in life. That second start begins at the breast, when the calf, piglet, puppy, or infant instinctively reaches for its first meal. Without it, mammals would cease to exist because the offspring would not get the essential nutrients, antibodies, and immune system enhancers they need to have a chance at living a healthy life.

We humans have upset this natural course. In our so-called "advanced" society, breastfeeding is not encouraged, and in fact it is often discouraged. Artificial formulas have replaced what Nature intended human infants to get from their mother. Bottle feeding is touted as being convenient, especially for working mothers. The decline in breastfeeding has had dramatic negative effects on the health of children in America and in other societies in which breastfeeding has taken a backseat to packaged formulas. For example:

• The more breast milk infants receive during the first six months of their life, the less likely they will be afflicted with diarrhea or ear infections, two of the most common and troublesome disorders in early childhood.(2)

• Infants who are only breast-fed and those who are breast-fed for at least three months have a significantly lower incidence of otitis media (middle ear infections) than infants who are not breast-fed. (3)

• Infants who are breast-fed are one-fifth to one-third less likely to die of sudden infant death syndrome. (4)

• Breast-fed infants are less likely to require hospitalization if they become ill, whereas infants fed formula are up to fifteen times more likely to need hospitalization when ill (5).

A revival of breastfeeding in the United States requires a shift in how Americans perceive it both as a social activity and as a health issue. One goal of the Health People 2000 project, run by the US Department of Health and Human Services, is to "increase to at least 75 percent the proportion of mothers who breastfeed their babies in the early postpartum period and to at least 50% the proportion who continue breastfeeding until their babies are 5 to 6 months old."(6) As the millennium closes, fewer mothers breastfeed their infants today than in the mid-1980s. According to Pediatrics, only 21.6 percent of mothers were nursing their infants six months after leaving the hospital, and many of them were also supplementing with formula.(7).

Physicians need to participate in the revival of breastfeeding. According to a survey conducted by the American Academy of Pediatrics of 1,602 of its active members, only 65 percent of the responding physicians recommended breastfeeding as the only feeding method during the first month after birth, and a mere 37 percent recommended it for one year.(8), which is the recommended length of time to breast feed, according to the American Academy of Pediatrics' position paper on breastfeeding issued in 1997.(9)

Why all this fuss about breastfeeding ? Because it is Nature's simple yet critical first gift to humans, and all mammals. Because it establishes invaluable emotional bonds between mother and child. Because it has been shown that breastfeeding mothers have a significantly reduced risk of developing breast cancer, ovarian cancer, endometrial cancer, and osteoporosis.(10) Because children who were breast-fed have higher IQs and less neurological dysfunctions than children who were not breast-fed.(11) Because breastfeeding can prevent a multitude of medical problems, problems which cost Americans a conservative estimate of $4.18 billion per year. (12)

But most of all, breastfeeding is important because it provides all infants, especially during those first critical feedings, with the first food they need to begin and establish their resistance to the hostile organisms that lurk everywhere in their new environment. These organisms can cause a long list of diseases and illnesses, including allergies, asthma, diabetes, diarrhea, gastrointestinal disorders, heart disease, rheumatoid arthritis, and many others that can plague them not only during infancy and childhood but through adulthood as well.

Infants are not the only ones who need colostrum, as you will see in the chapters that follow.

CHAPTER 2: WHAT IS COLOSTRUM?

DID YOU KNOW THAT...

• Bovine colostrum contains substances that are effective against many of the different microorganisms that are now resistant to the antibiotics on the market.

• Colostrum has anti-aging benefits, including the ability to reduce the occurrence of wrinkles.

• Colostrum is the only food that offers protection against invasion by bacteria, viruses, protozoa, fungi, and other disease-causing organisms.

It has been called mother's gold — colostrum, a thick, yellow substance that is produced toward the end of a female's pregnancy and is emitted by her mammary glands during the first 24 to 48 hours after giving birth. For human newborns, each of the first few breastfeedings provides the infant with colostrum. The amount of colostrum decreases with each successive time at the breast until the mother begins to provide pure breast milk the third day after birth. While humans produce small amounts of colostrum, a cow produces approximately nine gallons during the first thirty-six hours after giving birth.

Yet, whether it's teaspoons or gallons, Nature provides the right amount of this precious liquid for its intended recipient. Each drop contains the promise of life: the immunuglobulins, growth factors, antibodies, vitamins, minerals, enzymes, amino acids, and other special substances designed to "prime" the body to face a lifetime of invasion by various microorganisms and environmental toxins bent on destruction.

An infant's intestinal tract is ready to receive this special food. Scientists have discovered that during the first 24 to 36 hours of an infant's life, its intestinal wall has many large pores through which to receive the immunoactive molecules supplied by colostrum.(13) Researchers estimate that colostrum triggers approximately fifty processes in infants. To accomplish this, colostrum delivers some very special substances to infants, including:

• Immune factors, which facilitate the development of a strong immune system.

• Growth factors, which are essential in the creation and maintenance of bone, muscle, nerves, and cartilage, as well as other essential functions.

Colostrum *Nature's Healing Miracle*

• Antibodies (immunoglobulins) that protect the infant from invading organisms. Although having these antibodies is no guarantee the infant will not get sick, it can minimize the severity of an illness and does provide the ammunition needed to ward off and fight invading organisms, including those the mother's body produced for diseases she had before her pregnancy, such as measles, mumps, and pertussis. Antibodies also stimulate the infant's own immune system to create immunity to invasion by disease-causing organisms.

• A high level of protein and little fat. An infant's underdeveloped intestinal system is not prepared to process fats, so Nature provides the optimal ratio of protein and fat during this time.

Colostrum also acts as a laxative to help eliminate meconium, the first stools of a newborn, which are dark green and composed of mucus, bile pigments, and cellular debris.

Not only is colostrum a wonderful first food for infants, but adults can enjoy all its benefits too. Science has found a way to package the first food that comes from the udder of a cow and deliver it to you. Colostrum is not a drug; it is a safe, natural, non-allergenic food supplement that is rich in healing compounds. The colostrum eagerly awaited by newborn calves that gives them the strength and vitality to get to their feet within minutes of birth and allows them to fight off microorganisms that infest their world, is the same colostrum taken by humans to treat and heal dozens of conditions – plus help create new levels of vitality and well-being.

Who Can Take Colostrum?

Perhaps the question should be, who can't take colostrum? Adults, children and infants can all benefit from colostrum. Naturally, the ideal colostrum for newborns is what they get from their own mother, along with breast milk. Bovine colostrum is available in liquid or powder form, which can easily be added to an infant's formula. Use of bovine colostrum for infants may be a consideration if a mother is unable to breast feed, but it should be provided only with a physician's approval and supervision. If you are a new mother who cannot breast feed and you want to provide your infant with one of the best foods nature can offer, consult with your physician about the possibility of giving bovine colostrum to your child.

Unlike adults, children's bodies produce many of the immune and growth components found in colostrum, so it is not necessary to make colostrum a part of a regular supplement program for them unless they have a chronic problem, such as allergies or asthma. In other cases, colostrum is beneficial for children when they are coming down with or already have cold, flu, bronchitis, or other bacterial or viral infections, especially when antibiotics are the routine conventional treatment .

Adults young and old can reap the health advantages of colostrum, whether they have an existing illness or they want to take it as an insurance policy and to boost their energy level. Adults are prime candidates for bovine colostrum because once men and women pass puberty, production of immune and growth factors starts to decrease, and aging begins in earnest. So far, colostrum is the only natural supplement known that can deliver the right combination of growth and immune factors in a balanced, natural package, and in a form that is bioavailable to the human body.

HISTORY OF COLOSTRUM USE

Although it seems like colostrum recently burst onto the scene, it actually has a long history of use as a natural healer. For thousands of years, Ayurvedic physicians and the Rishis (sacred healers) in India have used bovine colostrum for both physical and spiritual healing. One Ayurvedic practice is to drop colostrum into boiling water and roll the balls in sugar. The Scandinavians and northern Europeans celebrate the health of a newborn calf (as well as contribute to their own health) by preparing and eating a pudding made with colostrum and honey.

In the United States, colostrum was used for its antibiotic properties before sulfa drugs and antibiotics were available. Physicians in the 1950s often prescribed it to treat rheumatoid arthritis. Albert Sabin, MD, the physician who discovered the polio vaccine, isolated the antipolio antibodies in bovine colostrum and went on to develop a successful vaccine in 1962.(14)

Since then there have been many studies of colostrum conducted around the world. Research has revealed a wealth of information about the healing potential of colostrum and its components and their ability to fight disease. Its healing powers were called into play in the mid-1980s when children with diarrhea caused by rotavirus were treated successfully with bovine colostrum.(15) Subsequent studies showed that it also protects children and adults against infectious diarrhea and diarrhea caused by the protozoa Cryptosporidium, especially in people who have weakened immune systems.(16)

George's Story

George of Pennsylvania didn't have any of this medical information when he first heard about colostrum. "My sister told me about colostrum and how it might help me, and I was skeptical at first." And he had every reason to be skeptical, because up to that point, no one in the world of medicine had been able to help him. To endure the rigors required of a firefighter, you must be in superb physical shape. And George was, until mysterious symptoms began to rob him of his ability to do his job. In February 1995, the insidious string of problems began with tingling and discomfort in his left calf and quickly progressed to thickening skin, discoloration, and severe pain when stooping. Despite visits with several specialists, no one could give him a diagnosis. In May 1995, George was forced to quit the job he loved because he could not endure the pain.

Although George had to quit, the disease did not. In September 1995, he finally got a diagnosis—linear scleroderma—a chronic, often fatal disease of unknown cause in which the skin progressively thickens and tightens, causing pain, restricted movement, and eventually affecting the internal organs as well. George needed prescription pain killers just to sleep at night. His leg had to be layered with petroleum jelly and wrapped with gauze to prevent infection. Despite his precautions, blisters still broke out and his leg often got infected. Treatment with oral and topical antibiotics left him exhausted and still in pain.

In March 1996, George's sister learned about colostrum and proposed that George try it. Like many people who live with pain and disease, he had heard stories about different "cures" and at first dismissed colostrum as just another false hope. Yet in the middle of May he decided he had nothing to lose. But he was wrong. "On the tenth day (after starting colostrum) I woke up to find that the pain in my leg was gone and the skin was not as hard." His doctor was 'astonished with the improvement' and "began to wean me off of the prednisone." George continued to take colostrum, which he credits with "reversing the damage to my leg. Without the colostrum, I feel that I would still be having serious problems with my leg. Colostrum may or may not be the cure for scleroderma, but it sure makes it easier to live with."

Supplements of bovine colostrum have helped tens of thousands of people who suffer with a wide variety of ailments and diseases. Many of them are like George: skeptical at first, cautiously optimistic when they start to take it, then pleased with the results. Inevitably at some point, the questions come up: Why bovine colostrum? What makes it so special? Why not take supplements of human colostrum?

Bovine vs. Human Colostrum

It's been said that cow's milk is made for calves and human milk is made for humans, and never the twain should meet. Indeed, the American Academy of Pediatrics' position paper on breastfeeding states that exclusive breastfeeding is the ideal source of nutrition for infants and should continue for at least 12 months, preferably longer. Infants who are weaned before the age of 12 months should not be given cow's milk but an iron-fortified formula instead.(17)

But colostrum is different. When it comes to colostrum, four interesting facts arise that make the bovine derivative an excellent candidate for supplementation for humans.

First , it is not species specific. That means it can be consumed safely by nearly every mammal, including humans. In particular, the molecular structure of the immune and growth factors in bovine colostrum is very similar to those found in humans.(18) In a sense, cows are universal donors of colostrum.

Second , bovine colostrum contains greater levels of some factors than does human colostrum. This fact is especially important for the immunoglobulin (a protein that acts as an antibody) called IgG. Dr. C.E. Bruce discovered that while human colostrum contains only 2 percent of this critical immunoglobulin, bovine colostrum contains 38 percent. (19) IgG is considered to be one of the body's most important immunoglobulins, because it is active against so many different microorganisms, many of which are now resistant to the antibiotics on the market. The increasing inability of antibiotics to fight common and often deadly microorganisms makes the use of colostrum of paramount importance in this fight we cannot afford to lose. (See Chapter 3, "Compromised Immune System" and Chapter 4, "Immunoglobulins.) So in a sense, bovine colostrum is even better for you than human colostrum!

Colostrum *Nature's Healing Miracle*

Remember, of course, that bovine colostrum supplements are primarily for adults and children; the first choice for infants is still human colostrum and breast milk.

Third, the quality of bovine colostrum can be controlled. A large number of dairy cows can be raised, monitored, and maintained in a controlled environment that allows for the production of uncontaminated, high-quality colostrum. A significant number of pasture-fed cows are needed to ensure a broad-base of immune and growth factors. The collection and processing procedures also can be regulated to ensure an optimal product.

Fourth, bovine colostrum contains special compounds called glycoproteins and trypsin inhibitors that prevent the digestive juices in the human stomach from destroying the immune and growth factors in the colostrum. Without these inhibitors, the healing powers of bovine colostrum would not be made available to the human body.

Using supplements of human colostrum is problematic. Aside from the moral and ethical complications arising from collection of colostrum from new mothers, there are issues concerning quality control. Because there is no way to regulate the quality of human colostrum produced (mothers' use of tobacco, alcohol, or other drugs during pregnancy the presence of HIV or active tuberculosis, for example), it would require testing of each and every sample, or every donor. All in all, bovine colostrum is the logical choice.

The Tapestry that is Bovine Colostrum

Although bovine colostrum has been used for centuries to treat various conditions, scientists did not begin to understand exactly how and why it works until the last few decades. Conducting the research has been like weaving a huge tapestry composed of many threads—in fact, bovine colostrum contains more than 80 (and some estimates are as high as 250) "threads," or substances. All of these are woven together, interlocking and working as one to provide a holistic healing experience.

The threads that make up the tapestry fall into two main categories — immune factors and growth factors—and several minor ones, and each category contains many components. At this point, a brief introduction to the main components will help you better understand the next chapter, "Why We All Need Colostrum," while we save the more detailed explanation of each factor for chapter 4, "Colostrum: Nature's Secrets Revealed."

Immune Factors

Immune factors are substances that help the body fight off the invasion and destructive power of bacteria, viruses, fungi, protozoa, and other disease-causing organisms. Some immune factors have very specific tasks, such as stimulating the production of one particular process or agent in the body, while others act in a more broad-based, general manner, providing protection for the entire immune system or to a significant portion of it.

Colostrum is the only food that provides the body with these critical, preventive and protective factors. Some of the most important immune factors found in bovine colostrum include immunoglobulins (the primary active components in bovine colostrum), proline-rich polypeptide (PRP), lactoferrin (a potent, natural antibacterial, antiviral, and anti-inflammatory substance), cytokines (cancer-fighting agents), enzymes, glycoproteins and trypsin inhibitors, lysozymes, lymphokines (includes cancer-fighting substances), oligo polysaccharides, and glycoconjugates. Researchers recently discovered that PRP is an immune system modulator, toning down the action of an overactive immune system which can sometimes attack its own host.

Growth Factors

Growth factors are compounds whose primary effects are to promote healing by building, maintaining, and repairing bone, muscle, nerves, and cartilage; to stimulate fat metabolism; to regulate protein metabolism during fasting; to maintain balanced blood sugar levels; to help regulate the brain chemicals that control mood; and to promote wound healing. A "bonus" effect of growth factors appears to be their anti-aging benefits, some of which include reduction of wrinkles and tighter, younger-looking skin.

Scientists have identified the following growth factors in bovine colostrum, which are discussed in more detail in chapter 4: epithelial growth factor (EGF), fibroblast growth factor (FGF), insulin-like growth factors I and II (IGF-I, IGF-II), and transforming growth factors (TGF A & B).

In the next chapter, you will learn how all the interconnected components in colostrum are completely compatible with your body and how they can benefit you.

DID YOU KNOW THAT...

- Virtually all disease-causing organisms previously considered easily treatable with antibiotics are now at least partially resistant to the antibiotics originally designed to destroy them.

- Everybody needs to enhance their immune system to help avoid the need for antibiotics and to counteract their immune-damaging effects. Colostrum supplies that enhancement.

- Colostrum can destroy cancer-causing agents and other toxins in the environment before they can damage your body.

- Colostrum contains growth factors that can help your body better utilize the food you eat and burn more fat.

"I started taking colostrum...[and] for the first time in five years I did not get sick during the fall seasonal change even though many people around me had colds, flu, sinus problems, and bronchitis," reports Lynn of Colorado. "Within three days of taking colostrum my hayfever disappeared," says Lewis of California. "Also my asthma has gone away...my knees stopped hurting [and] I have more energy." "I have been nearly symptom free," reports Lisa of Pennsylvania, who suffered with extreme fatigue. "Even my eczema disappeared for the first time in almost two years."

The reasons why we need colostrum are best reflected by those who are taking the supplement. They are people like you and me who are living in a world surrounded and influenced by many factors that are constantly compromising our immune system health. That's why Nikki-Marie Welch, MD, of Arizona says, "This nutritional supplement [bovine colostrum] has become a part of my routine immune-boosting protocol. I estimate that I prescribe colostrum to approximately one-third of all my patients."

One reason we need colostrum has already been noted: the decline in breastfeeding, which has robbed many adults and children of the valuable health-promoting components in colostrum and breast milk. But if having been breast-fed were the only criterion for people to be guaranteed a strong immune system and healthy life, then why do people who were breast-fed still get sick?

Except for the one thing over which you have no control—the genes which cause you to either have or develop particular medical conditions—you create or have a significant role in creating the harmful factors that adversely affect your health—circumstances that make the need for colostrum so imperative. Some of the most important factors are discussed below.

Overuse of Antibiotics

This specific use (abuse) of antibiotics is so important, especially when talking about the immune system, that it deserves top billing. That's because the antibiotics we had once hoped would "save" us from the dozens of infectious organisms that can infect us are rapidly becoming ineffective. Every year, American doctors prescribe more than 133 million courses of antibiotics to nonhospitalized individuals; every day, 190 million doses are given to hospitalized patients.(20). And every day more and more bacteria become resistant to the antibiotics originally designed to destroy them. Resistance to antibiotics has reached, in the words of James Hughes, director of the National Center for Infectious Diseases at the Centers for Disease Control and Prevention, "a serious global problem....It affects virtually all of the pathogens we previously considered easily treatable."(21)

Many experts believe this problem exists for this reason: According to the Centers for Disease Control and Prevention, about 50 percent of antibiotic prescriptions written for outpatients were not necessary.(22) A good example is the common cold. Millions of prescriptions are written for antibiotics to treat colds, yet antibiotics attack bacteria, not viruses, which are what cause colds. The groups hardest hit by the growing problem of antibiotic resistance are the ones least able to fight infection: children and the elderly.

People of all ages should enhance their immune system to help ward off disease, minimize the need for antibiotics, and to counteract their immune-damaging effects. Colostrum supplies that enhancement.

Environmental Factors

We are surrounded by a wide range of environmental factors that can have a detrimental effect on our health. The sun, for example, in excess, can cause sunburn and skin cancer. Pollutants and toxins are everywhere: from secondhand smoke to gasoline fumes; from bacteria in our water supply to carcinogens in our

shampoo—all can take a significant and cumulative toll on our health. Some, like cigarette smoke, cause cancer as well as lower our resistance to infectious organisms. Others are more direct: polluted water introduces harmful organisms directly to our intestinal tract. Colostrum has the ability to destroy toxins, carcinogens, and other harmful pollutants before they can damage our bodies.

Drug Use

This category includes over-the-counter, prescription (antibiotics have their own section; see above), and illegal drugs, as well as alcohol and caffeine. The negative effects drugs can have on your body and your immune system in particular are too numerous to mention. One look at the precautions on the label or the package insert of any drug gives you a good idea of the problems that can arise.

Alcohol reduces the body's ability to fight infection, causes cells to die, has a toxic effect on the liver, and depletes the body of vital nutrients. Pregnant women who drink alcohol run the risk of having a child with fetal alcohol syndrome, a condition characterized by behavioral problems, greatly reduced resistance to infection, and other health problems. Caffeine causes cell degeneration, disturbs liver function, hinders the immune system, and interferes with mineral absorption. All in all, drugs can place the immune system in a severely vulnerable position; colostrum can help bring it back.

Diet

The food you eat has a tremendous impact on your health. For example, the National Cancer Institute estimates that 35 percent of all cancer deaths are related to diet.(23) This figure does not include other diet-related diseases, such as diabetes, gastrointestinal disorders, osteoporosis, heart disease, malabsorption disorders (e.g., celiac), anemia, and leaky gut syndrome, a very common disorder which can lead to dozens of other conditions such as diarrhea, food allergies, Crohn's disease, and chronic fatigue syndrome. (See chapter 4 for a detailed discussion of leaky gut syndrome.)

The Standard American Diet (SAD) is exactly that: sadly high in fat, cholesterol, salt, sugar, and additives, and low in fiber, fruits and vegetables, and other whole foods. Although colostrum cannot replace the benefits of eating a healthy diet, it can help increase nutrient absorption, improve the effectiveness of nutritional supplements, and help cure leaky gut syndrome.

Obesity

Americans are fat and getting fatter, primarily as a result of poor eating habits and lack of adequate exercise. The National Health and Nutrition Examination Survey (NHANES; 1988-1994) found that one-third, or 58 million American adults ages 20 through 74, are clinically overweight. An analysis shows the percentage is highest among black and Hispanic women, of whom 50 percent are overweight.(24) Given that obesity is linked with so many serious diseases, such as diabetes, high blood pressure, heart disease, gallbladder disease, and stroke, safe, effective weight loss is of paramount importance for reasons of both health and self-esteem. Colostrum contains several factors, such as insulin-like growth factors and growth hormone, that help burn fat and build lean muscle mass.

The battle of the bulge is the longest running battle in history and has included the greatest number of casualties in the world. In a press release from the National Institutes of Health on 17 June 1998, it reported that 55 percent of Americans (97 million people) are obese.(30) Millions of Americans go on fad diets, only to become discouraged and often gain back any of the weight they lost, and often a few pounds extra as well.

Colostrum contains growth factors that can help your body better utilize the food you eat and burn more fat. These growth factors (in particular, IGF-1, or insulin-like growth factor I; see chapter 4) are normally produced by the body, but their numbers can be severely reduced by aging, lack of exercise, exposure to environmental toxins, and poor nutrition. Colostrum restores the body's levels of IGF-1 which, along with exercise and a nutritious diet, can result in better metabolization ("burning") of fat, increased rate of growth of muscle mass, and better strength and endurance — leading to a leaner, healthier body and appearance.

Colostrum *Nature's Healing Miracle*

Lack of Exercise

We have become increasingly sedentary, and the result is a population fraught with obesity, high blood pressure, heart disease, diabetes, and other diseases associated with a lack of activity. While taking colostrum can't make you exercise more, it can give you the added energy to want to be more active.

Contaminated Food

With every bite you take, chances are you are ingesting contaminants—pesticide residues, artificial food colorings, flavorings, and preservatives; and paraffin, beeswax, or other substances that coat fruits and vegetables. According to the Natural Resources Defense Council, 845 million pounds of pesticides, fungicides, and herbicides were used to treat crops in the United States in 1997, and imported foods are contaminated as well.(25) Another concern is the increasing occurrence of bacterial contamination of food, especially meat and dairy products, by bacteria such as E. coli, Listeria, and Salmonella. The US Department of Agriculture reports that as many as 3.8 million Americans a year are sickened by Salmonella-tainted food alone.(26) Overall, approximately 33 million Americans experience food poisoning each year, and more than 9,000 die of it!

Another area of food contamination is the use of antibiotics in animal feed. If you eat meat, the beef, chicken, pork, or lamb on your dish is delivering antibiotics to your system. Use of antibiotics in animal feed as a way to promote growth and fight infections among food animals is rampant. When you eat these animals, you ingest antibiotic residuals. These slowly build up in your system, increasing your need for more potent antibiotics if you should need to take the drugs. Plus, you'll get the other negative side effects of antibiotics: a weakened immune system, and partial or complete destruction of beneficial intestinal flora.

Stress

Researchers in the new branch of medical science called psychoneuroimmunology (psycho [mind]; neuro [nervous system]; and immuno [immune system]) have documented that emotional, physical, and environmental stress can break down the immune system and make you less resistant to colds, flu, and other infections. One of the hardest hit in the immune system are specialized cells called natural killer cells, which defend against viral infections and cancerous tumors.(27) Colostrum helps enhance the immune system and makes it better able to defend against in viral invaders and tumor growth.

Aging

You might think this belongs in the "have no control" category, yet although everyone ages, not everyone grows old. You can be a vibrant, trim ninety-six or a lethargic, obese forty-five. Use of colostrum, along with prudent lifestyle choices (including a nutritious diet, regular exercise, stress reduction, and other healthy habits), can significantly change how you age and prevent you from growing old. The growth factors in colostrum are especially effective as anti-aging agents (see chapter 4).

As in Nature, all things are related, some things more directly than others, yet all are part of the whole. Thus many of the factors mentioned above overlap when we discuss why we all need colostrum. Each one of us can identify with at least one of the following areas in which colostrum can make a difference in our lives.

Compromised Immune System

Everyone's immune system is compromised at one time or another because it is constantly being assaulted from all sides by any one of the factors mentioned above, and more. Such assaults invite the development of infectious and degenerative conditions, nearly all of which are associated and begin with a weakened immune system.

A key component of a healthy immune system is the bowel, or intestines. If the intestinal lining is unhealthy, that is, there are abnormally large gaps or holes between the cells in the intestinal wall, then harmful substances such as bacteria, parasites, viruses, and toxic substances can pass through the wall and into the bloodstream, trigger an immune response, and cause disease and complications. This condition, known as leaky gut syndrome, is very common and can play a critical role in your health. It is discussed in more detail in chapter 4.

When we feel good, we tend to take our body for granted. We eat junk food, work long hours, stay out too late, or become couch potatoes. But when a pathogen (an infectious organism; e.g., bacteria, virus) infiltrates and attacks our intestinal tract, giving us diarrhea or stomach cramps; or we get a cut or broken bone and infection sets in, we tune in to the pain. While we've been on "vacation," our immune system has been at work; in fact, it's always trying to protect us against disease-causing organisms. We often fail to realize that problems can be brewing within us without our knowledge, because we do not always have apparent signs or symptoms, like a fever, an abscess, or swollen joints. When the immune system is weakened by excessive antibiotic use, chronic deficiency of vitamins and minerals, exposure to toxins, or other assaults, diseases can develop over time and thrive, undetected, until they become serious.

How Colostrum Can Help

Colostrum is effective as both a treatment and a preventive measure for the immune system. It can prevent diseases and conditions such as colds, flu, diarrhea, sinusitis, asthma, allergies, herpes, viral bronchitis, candidiasis, and ear infections because it can boost underactive or weakened immune function. At the same time, it also can balance an overactive immune system, which is the situation for people who have an autoimmune disease (in which the body attacks its own healthy cells). Such conditions include fibromyalgia, lupus, rheumatoid arthritis, multiple sclerosis, and scleroderma, among many others. (See reference to PRP above).

What the Experts Say about Colostrum

When I first heard the claims about colostrum I dismissed them. Now, after seeing the research and seeing patients' results for myself, I'm a believer. My confidence in colostrum's abilities are shared by many of my colleagues. In hundreds of reports, physicians and researchers note their experiences with colostrum; a brief sample of their published findings and personal experiences is below.

• "Bovine colostrum could provide a novel, inexpensive approach for the prevention and treatment of the injurious effects of NSAIDs [nonsteroidal anti-inflammatory drugs] on the gut and may also be of value for the treatment of other ulcerative conditions of the bowel." (RJ Playford, et al, Gut 44 [5] [May 1999]: 653-658)

• "Treatment with antirotavirus immunoglobulin of bovine colostral [colostrum] origin is effective in the management of children with acute rotavirus diarrhea." (SA Sarker et al, Pediatr Infect Dis J 17 [12] [December 1998]: 1149-1154)

• "The colostrum-derived products contain...agents that promote anti-inflammatory...activity," and "the most valuable aspect of this new therapeutic alternative is its profound effect on pain relief." (A Nitsch and FP Nitsch, J Orthomolecular Medicine 13 [2] [1998]: 110-118)

• "Immunoglobulin in colostrum has been used to successfully treat: thrombocytopenia, anemia, neutropenia, myasthenia gravis, Guillain Barre syndrome, multiple sclerosis, systemic lupus, rheumatoid arthritis, bullous pamphigoid, Kawasaki's syndrome, chronic fatigue syndrome, and Crohn's disease, among others." (Dwyer, "Manipulating the Immune System with Immunoglobulin," N Eng J Med, 326 [Jan. 9, 1992]: 107).

• "Colostrum...helps fight herpes virus...[and] protects against the bacteria that cause stomach ulcers." (Raloff, Science News 147 [April 15, 1995]: 231).

• "Immunoglobulins (found in colostrum) are able to neutralize the most harmful bacteria, viruses, and yeasts." (P Brandtzaeg, Ann NY Acad Sci 409 (1983): 353-378)

• "Bovine colostrum [is] ... very effective in promoting wound healing. Recommended for trauma and surgical healing."

(Sporn et al, Science 219 [1983]: 1329-31).

• *"In my practice, patients who start taking colostrum when they are already ill with a viral or bacterial infection have greatly accelerated healing and recovery times." (Michael R. Joseph, DC, DACBN, CCN, Hawaii)*

• *"I've found that colostrum helps with problems that have not or cannot be addressed by any other methods. It has proven very effective in conditions of weakened immunity, or autoimmune conditions such as Epstein-Barr. It's also very helpful in helping patients with toxic conditions." (Carl Hawkins, DC, Utah)*

• *"In my practice, I use colostrum to manage a variety of conditions, including lowered immune function, chronic or recurring infections, autoimmune diseases, colds, flu, allergies, and prostatitis." (Nikki-Marie Welch, MD, Arizona)*

Colostrum and AIDS

People often ask about colostrum for the treatment of HIV/AIDS and cancer. The human immunodeficiency virus (HIV) is a rapidly mutating virus that quickly destroys the immune system's ability to fight it off. When this happens and patients develop AIDS (acquired immunodeficiency syndrome), their immune systems are in a highly compromised state, especially in the bowel. This leaves them wide open for all types of potentially deadly infections.

Chronic diarrhea is one of the most common symptoms experienced by AIDS patients. It can rapidly further reduce patients' ability to fight infection and deplete them of essential nutrients and body fluids. The result is a severe loss of weight (known as wasting), a process that can be stopped if the intestinal mucosa can be healed. Colostrum can not only eliminate the infectious pathogens and restore intestinal health but also prevent the diarrhea from starting in the first place.(28) In addition, the growth factors in colostrum, particularly insulin-like growth factor-I and growth hormones, help increase muscle mass, an important benefit for HIV/AIDS patients who are experiencing wasting.

Colostrum and Cancer

Cancer is an umbrella term for more than one hundred diseases whose common characteristic is uncontrolled abnormal cell growth. Many different factors can cause renegade cells, including heredity, smoking, exposure to environmental toxins, excessive sun exposure, food additives, pesticides, alcohol, and viruses. Colostrum provides components that enhance the immune system and help prevent the damage caused by these risk factors. Several factors present in colostrum have demonstrated particular promise in fighting cancer, including cytokines (which include the powerful cancer fighters interleukins), lymphokines, transfer growth factor B, and lactoferrin. Although more research needs to be done in the area of colostrum and cancer prevention, many studies have indicated great promise in the use of these substances against cancer (also see "Cytokines" in chapter 4).(29)

Effects of Aging

Here's a category none of us can escape. After adolescence, the body's production of growth hormones, which are needed for cell reproduction and maintenance, begins to decline steadily. By age 60, the body secretes little or no growth hormones, and aging accelerates rapidly. The immune system also starts to decline while we are still young so that by age sixty-five, function of the thymus gland and the T-cells (two key players in immune functioning; see chapter 4) are greatly reduced and the body's ability to respond aggressively and effectively to pathogens is about 50 percent of what it used to be. Other changes associated with aging, include wear and tear on the joints, loss of skin elasticity, decreased functioning of the endocrine glands with a resulting reduction in the number of circulating hormones, decreased output of insulin by the pancreas, and decreased activity by the adrenal glands (which are responsible for regulating the body's response to stress).

Yes, we do age, but we do not have to grow old. Colostrum supplies the body with growth factors (hormones) as well as stimulates the endocrine system to keep producing its own supply of hormones. Research strongly indicates that the combination of growth factors and immune factors found in colostrum work together to create a potent anti-aging effect. Some of those effects include tighter skin, which results in a reduction of wrinkles; and regrowth of cells and tissue of organs that normally decrease in size with age.

Overall Health Benefits

You may not have a pressing health issue you need to resolve, but colostrum can still offer you advantages. Colostrum provides "behind-the-scenes" health benefits, helping you maintain your energy level and well-being, and keeping your immune system in tune. Many people like to take colostrum as a preventive measure, and more and more doctors are recommending it to their patients.

"I think its use would be good for all people prophylactically," says Nikki-Marie Welch, MD, "and I suggest its use to any patient who needs that kind of immunological pickup."

"My patients taking colostrum report to me that they just don't get infections of any kind anymore," reports Brent Wells, DC, who practices in St. Louis, Missouri, and "their energy is better."

Michael R. Joseph, DC, of Hawaii, uses bovine colostrum "to stimulate the immune systems of older folks rather than have them take immune shots every year."(31)

Athletes are a good example of individuals who can greatly benefit from colostrum. Athletes are faced with a paradox: part of the reason they work out is to be healthy, yet they tend to be more susceptible to infections. The reason is that after a vigorous workout, the immune system temporarily reduces its production of T-cells and natural killer cells. This state of immune depression may last a few hours and then the system returns to its previous state. Some athletes continuously put themselves into this suppressed state, further increasing the chance they will become ill. Colostrum can help reduce the chance they may fall victim to opportunistic pathogens during their "down" time.

Bodybuilders also can gain some specific benefits from bovine colostrum. These athletes are always looking for ways to lose fat, build muscle, and gain strength. Colostrum contains the ingredients they are looking for: growth factors, including insulin-like growth factors IGF-I and II and growth hormone (GH). In fact, not only are the IGFs in cows and humans identical, but bovine colostrum contains a greater concentration of IGF-I than human colostrum.(32) This fact makes bovine colostrum attractive to bodybuilders, because according to a recent study conducted in Finland, IGF-1 induces protein synthesis, which helps improve overall performance.(33) Bovine colostrum also contains a truncated version of IGF-I that is ten times more potent than normal IGF-I.(34)

If you are an athlete, what can you expect from colostrum? IGF-I increases uptake of blood glucose and facilitates the transport of glucose to the muscles, which keeps energy levels up. Together with growth hormones, IGF-I also slows the rate of protein breakdown (catabolism) that occurs after a vigorous workout and speeds up protein synthesis, which results in an increase in lean muscle mass without an increase in the amount of stored fat. Colostrum also improves the assimilation of nutrients, which leads to improved energy levels and performance.

Colostrum: Your Second Chance

Sometimes it appears that the odds are stacked against us. We have upset Nature's natural rhythms by flooding our soil, water, air, and food with toxins, which in turn invade our body and disturb its natural state of health. We try to eat right and get enough exercise, but life's fast pace and demands often mean we eat fatty fast food, get little or no exercise, and pile on the stress. And then some of us are born with genes that predispose us to less than optimal health.

But Nature offers us another chance to restore our health and to create a healthy internal environment that continually promotes it. Colostrum provides that chance. And perhaps few people have been more grateful for that opportunity than Kaye in Arizona.

CHAPTER 4: COLOSTRUM: NATURE'S SECRETS REVEALED

DID YOU KNOW THAT...

- Colostrum's primary task is to go where it will do the most good—the immune system—and get it in order. Thus colostrum acts as both an insurance policy against disease and a treatment for the immune system and your health.

- The most convincing proof of the link between GI health and overall health is the existence of leaky gut syndrome. Fortunately, bovine colostrum is the ideal solution for this condition.

- The immunoglobulins in bovine colostrum provide unique protection against disease-causing bacteria and viruses.

Many of the people who have used colostrum and reaped its benefits say it's a "miracle" because it has significantly changed the quality of their lives. "I truly believe that [colostrum] will become known as the miracle food of the new millennium," says KWS of Florida, who credits colostrum, or what she calls her "fuel of premium gas plus," with two "miracles."

Miracle one concerned her yearly bouts with asthma. KWS needed steroids to keep going during those attacks—drugs that left her immune system severely compromised. After taking colostrum for only five days, her wheezing completely stopped. After three weeks she was able to stop all of her medication, and she "was back among the living."

Miracle two was a pleasant side benefit. An ankle injury from her younger days had caused her years of chronic pain and a grinding sensation in the bones. After taking colostrum, the pain and grinding disappeared.

Whether you believe colostrum to be a miracle in human terms, in Nature's terms it seems to come close. Consider this: colostrum is Nature's first food, a complex formula of at least eighty-plus substances, timed to be delivered during a very short period of time, precisely when it is most needed and where it will provide the most benefit. Colostrum's primary task: go where it will do the most good—the immune system—and get it in order. We've mentioned the immune system in previous chapters. What is it? How does it work? How does colostrum get it in order? Just what are the secrets of colostrum?

The Immune System

The immune system is a complex network of organs, proteins (antibodies, or immunoglobulins), glands, and special cells that encompasses the entire body. Its purpose is to safeguard the body against any "unfriendly" or enemy substances or actions that prevent or compromise the body's ability to function in a healthy manner. These enemy agents can include, but are not limited to, bacteria, viruses, stress, trauma, cancer, toxic chemicals, food additives, and secondhand smoke. The immune network has the following functions:

 • It protects against infections that can arise from injuries, such as cuts, fractures, and burns.

 • It protects the body against the damage caused by free radicals (highly charged, unbalanced molecules that cause damage to the body by pairing up with other damaging molecules, such as those from drugs, chemical toxins, or food additives). As more free radicals pair up with other harmful molecules, they damage the DNA, create more free radicals, and start various processes, such as cancer, aging, heart disease, or more than sixty other conditions. The damage caused by free radicals is called oxidation, and one way to prevent such damage is to get enough antioxidants in your diet and/or with supplements. Colostrum contains some potent antioxidants (see below).

 • It controls the rate of aging and the factors involved in the process.

 • It responds to substances that cause allergic reactions.

The immune system responds to invaders in two ways: humoral immunity and cell-mediated immunity.

In humoral immunity, the manufacture of soldier proteins called antibodies (immunoglobulins) is stimulated by the introduction of a foreign substance, called an antigen, into the body. Antigens can enter the body any number of ways; for example, in contaminated food, through a cut or an abrasion, via a catheter, or breathed into the lungs. Antibodies are specialists: they are produced to match up with specific antigens. Once antigens have entered the body,

Colostrum *Nature's Healing Miracle*

the antibodies that have been produced especially for them attach themselves to the surface of the antigens and eventually cause their death.

In cell-mediated immunity, an army of white blood cells with specialized functions moves in to protect the body. These cells are transported throughout the body via the lymphatic and circulatory systems. The number of soldiers in the immune system army is high, yet a healthy system can function well because all the cells communicate with each other and with other sites in the network, including the organs and the brain. An overview of each of the principal soldiers and their primary tasks is explained below.

Thymus. This is the master gland of your immune network. Located just above the heart, it secretes hormones, which regulate various immune system functions, and T-cells, which have a major role in the immune network. The thymus is very vulnerable to the damaging impact of stress, toxins, and chronic illness.

Skin. As the body's largest organ, it is the first line of defense against many pathogens.

Bone marrow. Several immune system cells are manufactured here, including B-lymphocytes (B-cells).

Lymphatic system. As part of the immune network, it consists of the lymph nodes, lymph fluid, and lymphatic vessels. This system removes toxins from the tissues.

Lymphocytes. These white blood cells are the main defenders of the immune network. They recognize invaders, assemble a defense, deploy the troops, and stop the defensive process once the invaders have been eliminated. There are several types of lymphocytes. T-lymphocytes (T-cells) and B-lymphocytes (B-cells) are the primary defenders. The T-cells are assisted by helper T-cells, which stimulate action; suppressor T-cells, which suppress action; and natural killer cells, which kill tumor cells. Other lymphocytes include monocytes and macrophages, which recycle the debris created in the immune network. Monocytes can transform into macrophages. Macrophages also identify pathogens, surround them, and assist the helper T-cells in selecting the best immune response to destroy the enemy. Two important chemical messengers of the immune network are the lymphokines and monokines, which help launch offensive and defensive immune reactions.

Thus colostrum provides the immune system with a wide array of elements that promote and maintain its health, including the all-important immunoglobulins, as well as PRP, cytokines, lymphokines, and many others, all of which are explained in detail further along in this chapter.

The Center of Health: The Bowel

The bowel may not be the most glamorous organ, but it is the foundation of health. To understand why, it's important to know that nearly 80 percent of all pathogens enter the body through or attached to mucosal surfaces; e.g., the sinuses, respiratory tract, mouth, gastrointestinal tract, and bile ducts, and that the largest of the mucosal surfaces is the gastrointestinal (GI) tract. The GI tract is also where most infectious organisms enter the body and where the antibodies and many different beneficial bacteria (yes, bacteria can be both good and bad, depending on the type) are produced and work to attack invading pathogens and stop diseases before they take hold.

There's a constant battle going on in your GI tract—enemies coming in and your standing army fighting them off (that is, when the GI tract is healthy and your army is properly armed). When your defenses are weak, which can occur for many reasons, such as antibiotic use, poor nutrition, environmental toxins, and stress (see chapter 3), the invaders can take over, and disease settles in. Yes, the bowel is definitely where the action is.

Colostrum contains many compounds of critical importance in human health. Yet they are of little or no value if they are not bioavailable (able to be used by the body), and if they do not act where they are most needed—the bowel. Numerous studies conducted over the past twenty-five-plus years show that bovine colostrum contains protease inhibitors that prevent the digestive enzymes in the human digestive tract from destroying the immunoglobulins in colostrum, thus allowing them to pass virtually unaltered into the bowel and to adhere to the mucosal surfaces and do their work. A recent study, conducted at Harvard Medical School, demonstrates that bovine immunoglobulins resist breakdown in the gastrointestinal tract and retain their ability to help prevent and treat diarrhea and colitis associated with Clostridium difficile.(35)

Proof of colostrum's bioavailability was first reported in 1975, when researchers in Amsterdam found that bovine colostrum con-

Colostrum *Nature's Healing Miracle*

tains a glycoprotein that protects the immune and growth factors from being destroyed by the digestive acids in the human stomach.(36) Their work was verified by later studies. In 1980, for example, Dr. David Tyrell discovered that most of the antibodies in bovine colostrum remain viable in the intestinal tract, and in the same year, Dr. Sandholm and colleagues reported that bovine colostrum is richer in inhibitors and immune factors than is human colostrum.(37) Thus the makings of a compatible healer and protector of the human immune system came to the attention of the medical community.

Much evidence shows the relationship between bowel health and overall health. One major clue is that many of the antibodies produced by the body are made in the intestinal tract at a site called Peyer's patches. The antibodies produced in Peyer's patches prevent disease on the mucosal membranes and in the circulatory system. Further evidence lies with the link between infections of the bowel and those in the lungs. Once colostrum is in the bowel, its immunoglobulins stimulate the production of antibodies in both the intestinal tract and the lungs.

But the most convincing proof of the link between GI health and overall health is the existence of leaky gut syndrome.

The Compromised Bowel: Leaky Gut Syndrome

"Leaky gut syndrome. Sounds like your stomach is full of holes, like a sieve, and is leaking out its contents." Not a bad definition from someone who had no idea what leaky gut syndrome is. Leaky gut is very common: at least as common as all the immune system diseases combined. (By the way, "gut" is synonymous with intestine or bowel; it is not the stomach.)

Leaky gut syndrome, or intestinal permeability, is a condition in which the intestinal lining is more permeable than normal, which means there are unusually large pores or spaces between the cells that make up the intestinal wall. This additional space allows toxic substances such as bacteria, viruses, parasites, and other harmful factors to enter the bloodstream and reach every part of the body. In a healthy gut, these toxins are eliminated.

One feature of leaky gut syndrome is that undigested fats and proteins can escape into the intestinal wall, resulting in allergic responses by the body. Food allergies develop from a leaky gut

Colostrum *Nature's Healing Miracle*

when the large protein molecules (from food with protein/amino acids) pass through the intestinal wall and are absorbed before they are completely metabolized. The immune system recognizes these proteins as invaders and creates antibodies against them. Eventually, whenever you eat that particular food, the body attacks the proteins, and a food allergy is born.

Leaky gut syndrome and the inflammation of the intestinal lining that accompanies it can be triggered by use of antibiotics, corticosteroids (e.g., prednisone), nonsteroidal anti-inflammatory drugs (NSAIDs, e.g, aspirin, ibuprofen), birth control pills, foods contaminated by parasites, molds, or bacteria (e.g., E. coli, Salmonella, Listeria), viruses (e.g., rotavirus, HIV), excessive intake of refined sugars, enzyme deficiency (e.g., celiac disease), caffeine, alcohol, food additives, surgery, and a decrease in blood supply to the bowel. In the case of long-term use of antibiotics, for example, the good bacteria in the gut are destroyed, leaving the body's number one site for production of antibodies virtually unprotected. Incoming pathogens meet no resistance, and the resulting inflammation leads to leaky gut syndrome. Symptoms that often accompany leaky gut are intestinal cramps, diarrhea, constipation, fatigue, bloating, and gas.

A very common cause of GI injury is the use of NSAIDs. In a recent study, colostrum helped prevent GI injury in patients taking the NSAID indomethacin.(38) This suggests that colostrum may also be effective in preventing GI damage caused by other NSAIDs, including aspirin and ibuprofen (e.g., Motrin, Advil).

Another feature of leaky gut syndrome and bowel inflammation is malabsorption of minerals, which leads to mineral deficiencies. These deficiencies occur because the special carrier proteins, which transport the minerals from your food and supplements from the intestine to the bloodstream, are damaged by the inflamed gut lining. A zinc deficiency caused by poor absorption, for example, can result in hair loss (alopecia areata), and magnesium deficiency is common among people with fibromyalgia, even when they take supplements of magnesium, because the gut allows the mineral to leak into the bloodstream. Mineral deficiencies can lead to osteoporosis, arthritis, heart disease, fatigue, memory loss, headache, inability to concentrate, and irritability.

The compromised immunity that characterizes leaky gut syndrome can cause many medical conditions. Diarrheal diseases, such as those caused by cryptosporidia and rotavirus, are among

Colostrum *Nature's Healing Miracle*

the most common and potentially fatal (in infants, and especially in third-world countries) conditions caused by leaky gut. Another common problem created by this syndrome is food allergies. Food allergies can begin in infancy, especially among infants who are not breast-fed or only breast-fed for a very short time. Research indicates that colostrum and continued breastfeeding maintains a healthy intestinal environment, which helps prevent the development of allergies and leaky gut syndrome.

Then there are the many other autoimmune diseases associated with leaky gut syndrome. Some of them include alopecia areata, chronic fatigue syndrome, Crohn's disease, diabetes, fibromyalgia, hives, irritable bowel syndrome (which appears to be much more common than previously recognized), inflammatory bowel disease, multiple sclerosis, polymyalgia rheumatica, Raynaud's disease, rheumatoid arthritis, scleroderma, Sjogren's syndrome, ulcerative colitis, and vasculitis. The association between leaky gut and these conditions is this: the antibodies created by the body in response to the toxic substances that leak into the bloodstream can attach to various tissues throughout the body and trigger inflammation. As the body pours more and more of these substances into the body, autoantibodies are created, and the inflammation becomes chronic. The type of autoimmune disease that can develop depends on the location of the inflammation. If it happens in the blood vessels, vasculitis (inflammation of the blood vessels) occurs. When inflammation affects a joint, rheumatoid arthritis can be the result. If the antibodies attack the gut, Crohn's disease or colitis can develop.

The far arm of leaky gut syndrome reaches still further. The inflammation in the gut damages an immunoglobulin known as IgA, which works in the healthy gut to protect against infection. Without the help of IgA, pathogens can escape into the bloodstream and infect any part of the body. Excessive pathogens in the bloodstream can overburden the liver, whose job it is to detoxify the body. An overstressed liver can result in confusion, loss of concentration, and other mental and cognitive problems.

Colostrum to the Rescue

Colostrum is the ideal solution for leaky gut syndrome. As a gastroenterologist, I find the ability of colostrum to help with this pervasive and widespread condition to be especially exciting Because colostrum reaches the gut while its components are still viable, its immunoglobulins and other factors can attack the offending pathogens in the intestines and prevent them from causing damage. The growth factors have anti-inflammatory action and also help repair damaged cells in the lining, decreasing cellular spacing, and thus preventing further leakage.

For individuals who already have a disease associated with leaky gut syndrome, colostrum is a critical part of the healing process. Unless the gut is healed, the body will not begin to repair the damage that began with the source of the problem—the permeable gut. As healing begins, the amount of toxins dumped into the bloodstream from the gut will decline. Nutritional uptake will improve, the cells will have better access to the fuel they need to perform repairs and to reproduce, organ function will improve, and energy levels will rise. For optimal results, treatment with colostrum should always be accompanied by a nutrient-rich diet that eliminates sugar, white flour products, high-fat foods, caffeine, alcohol, grains that contain gluten (e.g., wheat, barley, rye), and dairy products for a long period of time, and hidden food allergies should be identified by a physician.

NOTE: Leaky gut syndrome is often not recognized by physicians. If you suspect you may have leaky gut syndrome or you have one of the conditions associated with leaky gut, there are several noninvasive diagnostic tests your physician can do.

Threads in the Tapestry: Components of Colostrum

We've already mentioned many of colostrum's components and noted some of their functions. To learn more about them, here is a detailed list and description of the primary ingredients in bovine colostrum.

Immune Factors

Immunoglobulins, or antibodies, are the most important and most prevalent immune factors in bovine colostrum. Immunoglobulins are found in all mammals, including humans, and are divided into five classes designated as IgA, IgD, IgE, IgG, and IgM. Each of these immunoglobulins has its own individual functions, but overall they neutralize toxins, viruses, and bacteria in the circulatory and lymphatic systems.

Colostrum *Nature's Healing Miracle*

Immunoglobulins (sometimes called immunoglobins and gammaglobulins) are made of chains of large protein molecules composed of hundreds of amino acids. Immunoglobulins work separately and together to destroy antigens. Some circulate in the blood and lymphatic systems; others reside in the mucous membranes and act as a barrier against invaders.

Immunoglobulins are of critical importance because bacteria are becoming increasingly resistant to antibiotics, deadly bacteria infect our food supply, new viruses are multiplying faster than the vaccines to combat them, and bacterial infections are being linked with more diseases, including peptic ulcers and heart disease. In fact, the relationship between bacterial infection and heart disorders has strong evidence to support it.(39) Colostrum and its rich supply of immunoglobulins may play a major role in combating this serious health problem.

The immunoglobulins in bovine colostrum provide unique protection against virtually all disease-causing organisms. It is unique because the levels of immune factors in bovine colostrum are ten to twenty times greater than those found in human colostrum. Why? Human infants receive about half of their immunity from their mother through the placenta. Calves, however, receive all of their initial immunity from colostrum, which means bovine colostrum needs to be incredibly high in immune factors. Those factors make it effective against many disease-causing organisms.

Your body can make good use of those immunoglobulins. As you read previously, the majority of your immunoglobulins are manufactured in the bowel. Bovine colostrum delivers its immunoglobulins to the bowel. It's a perfect match. Take IgG, for example. This is the most abundant immunoglobulin in bovine colostrum, and it is a key factor in the prevention and treatment of infectious diarrhea.(40) Ideally, physicians use IgG to combat various other conditions, including anemia, chickenpox, chronic fatigue syndrome, hepatitis, multiple sclerosis, neutropenia, and systemic lupus.

Lactoferrin is a protein that binds with iron and has antiviral, anti-bacterial, and anti-inflammatory action. It defends the body against candidiasis, cancer, chronic fatigue syndrome, herpes, and other infections.(41) Lactoferrin has a unique way of killing bacteria and supplying the body with iron at the same time. Bacteria need iron to reproduce. Lactoferrin attaches to iron and prevents bacteria from using it for their reproductive functions. Lactoferrin then gives the iron to the red blood cells, where it promotes a process that provides oxygen to the body's cells.

While lactoferrin is attached to bacteria, it also causes the bacterial membrane to become more porous, which allows the body's immune factors to more easily destroy the pathogens. Lactoferrin's anti-inflammatory activity is effective in vision disorders, while its antivitral properties help in the prevention and treatment of herpes, HIV, chronic fatigue syndrome, and other viral diseases. It also has shown promise against candida albicans, the yeast disorder that affects the lives of so many women.

Proline-rich Polypeptide (PRP) regulates the kingpin of the immune network, the thymus gland, which produces T-cells. It also serves a critical role in regulating autoimmune disease by balancing the immune system response and toning down the overreaction that characterizes autoimmune disease. It does this by inhibiting overproduction of T-cells and lymphocytes, which leads to a reduction in pain and swelling.

Lysozymes are potent hydrolyzing substances (agents that combine with water to produce a reaction) that enhance the function of the immune system. This compound is now added to infant formula to increase immune capability. Lysozymes are typically found in saliva, tears, and perspiration and are highly deadly to bacteria and viruses.

Cytokines are chemicals that are involved in cell-to-cell communication, antiviral and anti-tumor activity, and regulation of the duration and intensity of immune responses. They boost the activity of T-cells and stimulate production of immunoglobulins. Cytokines are composed of substances called interleukins, which scientists have numbered for convenience. One of them, interleukin-10, is a potent anti-inflammatory agent, which is useful for people with arthritis and other inflammatory disorders.(42) In a study conducted by Alejandro Nitsch, MD, and Fabiola Nitsch, MD, in which they gave colostrum to patients with rheumatoid arthritis and osteoarthritis, the doctors concluded that "the colostrum derived products contain…agents that promote anti-inflammatory cytokine-type activity," and that "the most valuable aspect of this new therapeutic alternative is its profound effect on pain relief."(43) Another, interleukin-2, has been used to treat some

forms of cancer.(44)

Glycoproteins and Trypsin Inhibitors help protect the immune and growth factors in colostrum from being destroyed by the digestive juices in the human gastrointestinal tract. Without these factors, bovine colostrum would not be effective in humans. Researchers have found that these inhibitors can prevent Helicobacter pylori from adhering to the stomach wall. Helicobacter pylori are bacteria responsible for causing peptic ulcer, gastric ulcer, and gastric cancer.(45)

Lymphokines are hormone-like peptides that regulate the immune system response. Tumor necrosis factors are one type of lymphokine.

Oligo polysaccharides and Glycoconjugates are sugars that attract and bind to various pathogens and prevent them from entering or attaching themselves to the intestinal mucus membranes. With the assistance of other colostrum components, these sugars block the attachment of many disease-causing organisms, including Streptococcus pneumococci, E. coli and Salmonella, Entomoeba, Cryptosporidia, Giardia, Shigella, Clostridium difficile toxins A & B, and others.

Other immune factors in bovine colostrum include alpha 2-AP glycoprotein, alpha 1-antitripsin, alpha 1-fetoprotein, alpha 2-macroglobulin, albumin, B lactoglobulin, beta 2-microglobulin, C3, C4, enzymes, haemopexin, haptoglobin, lactoperidoxase, orosomucoids, orotic acid, and prealbumin.

Growth Factors

Epithelial Growth Factor (EGF) is a protein substance that is instrumental in protecting and maintaining the skin. In 1983, researchers discovered that bovine colostrum contained EGF as part of a compound that also consisted of insulin-like growth factor I and transforming growth factors A & B.(46) Although EGF alone can stimulate normal skin growth, it performs best when combined with IGF-1 and TGF A&B. Together they stimulate normal skin growth and repair cellular tissue.

Fibroblast Growth Factor (FGF) performs a helper function by increasing the binding ability of IGF-I by 60 to 70 percent.

Insulin-Like Growth Factor I and II (IGF-I & IGF-II) are the most abundant growth factors in bovine colostrum. These proteins affect how the body uses fat, protein, and sugar; stimulate the immune system; and promote cell repair and growth. IGF-II is much more potent than its partner.

Because every cell in the body has a receptor for IGF-II, this growth factor can help each cell actively heal or reproduce. In particular, IGF-I is one of the few substances known that can stimulate the repair and growth of DNA and RNA, the all-important nucleic acids that are the "intelligence" of cells. DNA is the basis of heredity and contains the genetic information; RNA controls protein synthesis and carries messages to other cells in the body. These healing properties make IGF-I one of Nature's most powerful anti-aging substances.

Bodybuilders are interested in IGF-I because it can stimulate muscle growth and it does not promote fat storage (see "Other Health Benefits" in chapter 3). There is also evidence that IGF-I lowers LDL cholesterol levels (the "bad" cholesterol) and raises HDL cholesterol (the "good" cholesterol), which can help prevent heart disease.

True to its name, IGF-I has an effect on insulin, which is good news to people who have diabetes. A 1990 study showed that IGF-I may be an effective alternative to insulin in the transport of glucose to muscle, thus serving as an acute treatment of hyperglycemia and, for some people, reducing the amount of insulin they need to take daily. These benefits do not apply to diabetics who are obese, however.(47) IGF-I also benefits the immune system by stimulating production of T-cells.

Transforming Growth Factors A&B (TGF-A&B) stimulate proliferation of cells in connective tissue, assist in the formation of bone and cartilage, help repair tissue, and, according to one study, support the development of growth of the gut lining, which is important in leaky gut syndrome.(48)

Other Components

Bovine colostrum also contains the antioxidants vitamins A and E as well as vitamin B12 and traces of all other vitamins. The mineral sulfur is also found in colostrum. Sulfur is involved in many bodily processes, including metabolism, tissue repair, and the making of collagen (the primary component of cartilage and connective tissue), new cells, and new tissue.

DID YOU KNOW THAT...

> • **Colostrum's effectiveness is reduced if it isn't processed in such a way as to protect its relatively fragile immune and growth factors.**

> • **True colostrum contains extremely small amounts of lactose, which means that if you are lactose intolerant, you should not experience any problem with colostrum.**

> • **Colostrum from pasture-fed cows can transfer immunity to a wider range of disease-causing organisms.**

You've read a lot about what colostrum is and what it can do for you. What you haven't learned yet is how colostrum gets from the cow to you.

No one can improve on Nature's perfection, especially with something as complex as colostrum. But bovine colostrum can be packaged in forms that ensure you will receive all the wonders that Nature intended.

To tell you about those forms, we will explain the processes that make sure you get the most potent and viable colostrum. Why is this information important? Because if you take colostrum that has been processed improperly, you may as well not take it at all. You'll just be wasting your time and money and be no closer to resolving the problem for which you choose colostrum in the first place.

Colostrum's effectiveness is reduced if it isn't processed in such a way as to protect its relatively fragile immune and growth factors. But before we even get to the mechanical processing, let's consider the raw ingredients and the reservoir of those ingredients, the cow.

Where It All Begins: The Cow

The stomachs of the cow are the first "processing plant" for colostrum. To help ensure a pure, unadulterated end product, the cows selected to provide colostrum should be pasture-fed on grass that has not been treated with any type of pesticide, herbicide, or fungicide. They should not be subjected to courses of antibiotics, steroids, and growth hormones as are most other food and dairy cows. These substances contaminate the colostrum and milk of cows and, in addition to posing potential health risks to those who ingest the milk or colostrum, render the colostrum less effective.

When cows feed on naturally raised pasture, they are exposed to a natural variety of disease-causing substances, which then allows the cows to develop natural immunity to a wide variety of organisms, which is then passed along in their colostrum. They also get live enzymes and natural nutrients not found in dried feed. Thus organically grown grass is believed to be the optimal feed for cows selected to contribute colostrum. Cows that are not pasture-fed but given dried, processed feed do not develop the wide range of immunity-boosting components available from cows that are fed the food Nature intended.

Such dairy farms exist both in the United States and in other countries around the world. The country with some of the strictest standards for dairy farming is New Zealand. Dairy farmers in New Zealand are fined up to $100,000 if any of their dairy products contain a residue of pesticides, antibiotics, heavy metals, hormones, or chemicals. Thus many people consider New Zealand dairy cows to be the cleanest "factories" for colostrum.

John Heinerman, PhD, a medical anthropologist and author of more than 55 books, believes that "Unquestionably, patients victimized by colitis, gastroenteritis, heartburn, diverticulitis, Crohn's disease, and other such disorders do experience improved management of their GI tract when colostrum is taken in the form of New Zealand-sourced powder or capsules."(49)

To Market, To Market

Fire and ice—these two elements are the enemies of colostrum. Moderation is the key. The optimal way to process colostrum is to refrigerate (NOT freeze) the fresh colostrum.. Only low heat should be used during processing. New evidence suggests that use of indirect electric heat, rather than direct gas heat, is the best method for pasteurizing colostrum, as the latter approach can result in nitrate and nitrite residues in the product. Unfortunately, most colostrum produced in the U.S. is pasteurized using direct gas heat. This is part of the history of colostrum production in this country—until very recently, most colostrum produced in North America was targeted for the animal husbandry industry, and was not intended for human consumption. During the cooling process, colostrum needs to be stirred constantly so it will not gel. If it should gel, it makes it impossible to remove the fat, whey, and lactose, or to dry the colostrum properly.

Colostrum *Nature's Healing Miracle*

Many manufacturers—and virtually all U.S. manufacturers--freeze colostrum because it makes it easier to store and transport for processing . When colostrum is frozen, its molecular structure changes. The result is colostrum that is not water soluble, which in turn makes it very difficult for it to be assimilated by the body and disseminated in the bowel. This process also causes damage to the protein structures in colostrum, which is significant because these protein chains are the "home" of many of colostrum's important immune factors. Many experts believe, therefore, that the biological activity and effectiveness of colostrum that has been frozen is greatly reduced.

High-quality colostrum should be 100% colostrum, devoid of colostrum whey, milk whey, lactose, or fillers. Whey is a byproduct of milk and colostrum, and it is processed using heat and hydrochloric acid, two factors you definitely do not want associated with your colostrum supplement. True colostrum contains extremely small amounts of lactose, which means that people who are lactose intolerant usually do not experience any problem with colostrum (see chapter 6).

CHAPTER 6: HOW TO BUY AND USE COLOSTRUM

DID YOU KNOW THAT...

- Everyone can benefit from colostrum—infants, children, young adults, and the elderly.

- Colostrum is a nontoxic, nonallergenic food supplement that has no negative interactions with drugs, food, or other supplements.

- As a consumer, you have a legal right to see the independent evaluations performed on any supplement you buy so you can confirm its quality or lack of it.

If you were a calf, you'd be nuzzling up to an udder to get your colostrum. Fortunately, this isn't necessary, but if you get colostrum that's been processed properly (see Chapter 5), you'll still get all the benefits.

Shopping for Colostrum: A Checklist

Any colostrum product you buy should be completely water-soluble or contain water-soluble colostrum. Other standards you need to consider when shopping for colostrum are listed below. You want colostrum that has been:

- Refrigerated but NOT FROZEN (processed fresh).

- Derived from cows that have been pasture-fed (preferable but not necessary) and which are certified to be free of hormones, pesticides, and antibiotics.

- Collected from the first 1-5 milkings after the cow's second birthing, which ensures high-quality biological activity.

- Collected from a pool of thousands of cows, which provides you with standardized and maximized immune and growth factors.

- Filtered and homogenized, and when it's pasteurized, done so at minimum heat for the minimum amount of time to minimize the breakdown of the long-chain proteins (immunoglobulins), so you can better assimilate the product.

• Tested by a certified laboratory for the presence of pesticides, heavy metals, antibiotics, and disease-causing pathogens, such as salmonella and E. coli.

• Tested by a certified laboratory to ensure that it has a high platelet count (an indication that it has adequate numbers of "good" intestinal bacteria).

• Processed for the removal of excess fat, whey, and lactose and dried without the use of excessive heat. This type of processing is more time-consuming and more expensive than the high-temperature method, but the result is high-quality colostrum.

• De-fatted to ensure long shelf life. Full-fat colostrum becomes rancid fairly quickly.

• Gathered and processed by a dairy production company that is certified by the appropriate government agency – for example, the USDA in the United States or the Ministry of Agriculture and Fisheries in New Zealand. Most U.S. colostrum is processed by the veterinary industry and is not intended for human consumption.

For now, colostrum from New Zealand is considered by many experts to be the premier source. However, this may change as several U.S. manufacturers are improving their processing procedures. Be informed. As a consumer, you have the right to ask questions about the supplements you buy and to see the independent evaluations performed on them so you can confirm their quality or lack of it. The manufacturer is required to supply this information to you at your request. The manufacturer's name, address, telephone number, and/or website address should be on the label.

On The Shelf: Which Ones To Choose, Which Ones to Avoid?

Colostrum is available in a variety of forms; however, not every form provides optimal benefit. Here is an explanation of the different forms, their pros and cons, and how they are used.

• Capsules. Colostrum capsules are a recommended form to take. There are several types of capsules on the market. Bovine gelcaps reportedly dissolve best and allow the colostrum to most efficiently enter the bowel. This type of capsule is generally more expensive than other gelatin or vegetable-based capsules, which may not dissolve adequately in the bowel. Capsules are virtually tasteless and odorless and can be swallowed with water. If you prefer not to swallow the capsules, you can break them open and sprinkle the contents into food (applesauce, pudding, and yogurt work well) or mix the powder in water or juice and drink it. Make sure you drink enough water (see "How To Take Colostrum" below).

• Powder. The powdered form is another recommended way to take colostrum. It can be mixed with water (you still need to drink 8 to 12 ounces of water with the powder) or mixed in with applesauce, yogurt, or other foods. Athletes often like to mix the powder into their protein drinks. The powder also can be used to make a paste to treat skin wounds (see Chapter 8).

• Tablets. Tablets are typically cheaper to produce than capsules, so many manufacturers prefer to make them. But there are several ways to produce tablets, and choosing the right one is important. Hard pressed tablets are subjected to high temperatures during manufacturing, which destroys the biological activity of colostrum's growth and immune factors. Avoid these products unless you want to waste your time and money. Some tablets are pressed using virtually no heat or excessive pressure and therefore preserving the bioavailability of colostrum's components. If you want to buy tablets (and there are flavored tablets on the market which are especially targeted for children), make sure the package notes how the tablets were made and buy only those that have been cold pressed or pressed with very little heat or pressure.

• Liquid. Liquid colostrum is preferred by some people, especially those who find it difficult to swallow capsules. It is highly assimilable and particularly helpful for people who have digestive disorders or who are administering it to infants. Look for nonpasteurized colostrum that contains no preservatives, has been sterilized using microfilitration, and is vacuum-packed. If preservatives have been added to the colostrum, they dilute and compromise the potency of the supplement. Nonpasteurized colostrum needs to be refrigerated after opening and usually should be consumed within 30 days of breaking the seal. Liquid colostrum can be taken straight or mixed

Colostrum *Nature's Healing Miracle*

with juice or distilled water.

• **Foods** . **You can supplement your regular colostrum usage with certain food products that contain colostrum. These include snack bars, kefir, yogurt, and protein drinks. These products come in several flavors and are especially popular with children, athletes, and people who are always on the run. Look for brands that have at least 1,000 mg colostrum in each serving, are low-fat and have no cholesterol, preservatives, artificial colors or flavors, sucrose, or hydrogenated oils.**

How to Take Colostrum

The most beneficial amount varies from person to person. For preventive and maintenance purposes, many adults take three capsules twice daily (480 to 500 mg each capsule) or a combination of capsules and powder for the same number of milligrams. Always take colostrum on an empty stomach (generally, at least two hours after eating) and with 8 to 12 ounces of water to allow it to reach the upper intestines as quickly as possible. Refrain from eating for about 20 minutes after taking colostrum.

Recommended Usage

When treating a specific ailment or disease, the recommendation is to start with a high dosage (a practice called "front loading") of four to six capsules (about 2,000 to 3,000 mg) twice a day and then reduce the dosage to five capsules daily, in divided doses (e.g., three capsules in the morning and two in late afternoon), when you get your desired results. If you are also taking other supplements, take them 20 to 30 minutes before or after taking colostrum.

NOTE: A general rule with colostrum is that if you are not getting the results you want, increase the dosage gradually until you do. Once you get results, stay at that dosage level. Colostrum should be taken twice daily. Consistent use of colostrum provides the best results, as its benefits are cumulative.

There may be occasions when a different dosing schedule suits you better. Dr. Welch, for example, explains that she normally takes four capsules daily for maintenance. However, when she is exposed to infection, such as from a contagious patient, or she feels a cold or gastrointestinal symptoms coming on, she increases her dosage up to twelve capsules a day, taking two capsules every three hours for a few days. Brent Wells, DC, a chiropractic nutritionist and kinesiologist, recommends that his patients take four capsules twice daily initially, then reduce the dosage to one or two capsules twice daily. Dosing for children is proportionately less and should be based on the child's age and weight.

Capsules vs. Powder

Since capsules and powder are the two preferred forms of colostrum, which one should you take? The answer is, it depends on the reason for which you are taking the supplement. If you want to increase your energy level, burn fat, or improve healing, take any of the forms of colostrum. If, however, you want the benefits of the immune factors, take capsules on an empty stomach along with lots of water, to encourage distribution of the immune factors in the intestinal tract. Many people choose to take both capsules and powder—one form in the morning and the other later in the day—and reap the benefits of both.

Side Effects and Precautions

No substance is completely benign—even water, if taken in excess, can cause problems. Most people who take colostrum do not experience any side effects. Those who do report mild, temporary symptoms such as headache, muscle ache, stomach distress, or itching. These symptoms usually disappear after a day or two.

If you are pregnant or breastfeeding, consult your physician before taking colostrum. Also, if you have any of the following medical conditions, talk with your doctor before beginning colostrum, as it can affect the disease course: thyroid disorders, immune system disorders, or cancer.

You may experience some insomnia if you take colostrum late in the day. That's because colostrum can boost your energy level, which is welcome during the day but not necessarily before you retire.

Even though colostrum contains virtually no lactose, in rare cases, people who are lactose intolerant experience a reaction. Dr. Welch reports that although the amount of milk in bovine colostrum supplements is negligible, her experience has been that a small percentage of people experience gastrointestinal distress in the form of "gas" or bloating.(50) This can be due to several factors – toxins creating gas "on the way out" or "die-off" of yeasts and fungi such as Candida albicans. Some gastrointestinal discomfort when first taking colostrum is not necessarily a reason to discontinue it. It can also be alleviated by drinking more water with the colostrum. If you have these symptoms, consult your health care practitioner and keep taking the colostrum. If the symptoms persist for more than 3 or 4 days, consider stopping taking colostrum and trying it again at a later date.

CHAPTER 7: COLOSTRUM AND YOU

All of the information, statistics, and rhetoric in the previous chapters will mean nothing to you unless you take action. This is more than a story about colostrum—it is a story about people like yourself, individuals who are in search of health and natural healing. Some of those people tell their own stories here, stories about how taking colostrum changed their lives. For some it was a dramatic change; for others it was significant enough to make the quality of their lives much better. And we will not lie to you: 100 percent of the people who take colostrum do not sing its praises. Some do not take enough; others do not take it long enough. In many cases, people are taking colostrum supplements that have been processed and packaged in ways that have rendered them weak or ineffective. If colostrum is going to help you at all, it must be in a form your body can use. Anything less is a waste of your time and money, and it robs you of the opportunity to enhance your health and lifestyle. Be sure to follow the purchase and use recommendations in Chapter 6.

Arthritis

"Be patient and colostrum's health results will astound you and bring you joy and happiness." With these words, Jack explains that colostrum saved him from "a long history of health problems, most significantly, severe arthritis, sinus and hayfever." Relief did not come overnight for Jack. Indeed, everyone who takes colostrum heals at a different rate: some within hours or days; others weeks or months. Jack fell into the latter category. "I have learned that if it takes five years to get sick, it could take possibly five months to get well." But his patience paid off. After going through a few ups and downs, Jack reports that "colostrum has made such a great difference in my overall health that I advise everyone to take colostrum."

Asthma, Allergies

"I haven't felt this great in twenty years!" Twenty years was more than half the lifetime of thirty-six-year-old Debi of Kentucky, who had suffered from asthma, allergies, and skin disorders since the age of sixteen. She had nothing but more of the same to look forward to until she tried colostrum. With the words "I admit I was skeptical. But now…" she found relief not only for her asthma and

allergies but also the disturbing and unsightly skin eruptions and broken veins that plagued her over the years. An added bonus has been the disappearance of the daily fatigue that had accompanied her respiratory problems since adolescence.

Kirby reports that he had "immediate relief from allergies" after taking bovine colostrum. Before he took colostrum, he needed to take allergy shots daily so he could work his farm. "With colostrum, I no longer need shots and I'm free from suffering for the first time in my life."

Bronchial Pneumonia

Bronchial pneumonia is not pleasant for anyone, but when you're only fourteen months old, it is also scary, especially for the parents. Julia's daughter had been given several courses of antibiotics; two of which didn't work at all, and a third which caused an allergic reaction. That's when they tried colostrum. "We started giving her two colostrum capsules, twice a day. In three days, we saw a significant improvement and cut back to one capsule, twice daily. In just one week, her doctor's office visit revealed clear lungs and her asthma medication was no longer needed." Julia has continued to give her daughter one capsule a day, and since then she has not had any recurring respiratory problems.

Candida

Colostrum made it possible for Bernard to rid himself of a severe Candida infection he had for thirteen years. "I have used a lot of products to remove candida but they never solve my problems with properly digesting my food," he says. "The colostrum has made it possible for me to digest my food and has alleviated the constant pain in my abdomen."

Cellulitis

An eighty-two-year-old woman with severe cellulitis needed hospitalization, but she vehemently refused all conventional medical intervention. Her physician, Dr. Nikki-Marie Welch, treated her with topical bovine colostrum as well as oral doses. "The cellulitis cleared beautifully within two weeks," reports Dr. Welch.

Colitis

A sixteen-year-old boy who was being treated unsuccessfully for colitis was given bovine colostrum by chiropractic nutritionist and kinesiologist Brent Wells, DC. Before starting the colostrum, the patient was unable to keep food down and was suffering with diarrhea and stomach cramps. After only two weeks of taking colostrum, "he found himself eating normally with no pain, and no more diarrhea," reports Dr. Wells.

Diabetes

George had experienced severe pain in his left leg ever since he had back surgery in 1991. His doctors told him he had irreversible nerve damage, unwelcome news to anyone, but especially for a person who has insulin-dependent diabetes. The pain made it very difficult to walk. Two weeks after George started taking eight capsules of colostrum a day, he stopped taking his pain pills. "My doctor is amazed," says George. "Since taking colostrum, I have been able to reduce my insulin from 32 units a day to 20 units."

High Cholesterol

Kay had a high cholesterol level, but was unable to handle conventional medications. Then she heard about colostrum. "After taking it for a while, my cholesterol level dropped from 319 to 226. My doctor was very pleased and told me to continue taking it."

Multiple Sclerosis

"I cannot say enough good things about this miraculous food," says Bonnie of Utah. For seven years she had suffered from multiple sclerosis, experiencing vision problems, muscle weakness, fatigue, dizziness, and burning sensations in her feet. After taking three teaspoons of colostrum powder a day for several months, all of her symptoms disappeared. "I am able to walk without a limp and climb stairs without the aid of a railing," she says. "I feel like I have truly found a miracle in my life."

Lisa in Pennsylvania began taking colostrum for her multiple sclerosis and noticed that she felt stronger and had less fatigue.

Then she increased her dose and, she reports, "after one month, 95 percent of my symptoms are gone."

People of All Ages

Age is no barrier when it comes to colostrum. It certainly was no barrier for a seventy-nine-year-old man with hepatitis C, says Dr. Welch. At first she prescribed oral colostrum, which resulted in an improvement in symptoms. As an added benefit, the crusty lesions that had covered the forearms of the man also began to clear up. Dr. Welch added topical colostrum to the regimen, and the lesions disappeared. Although the type and cause of the lesions was never known, it seemed their disappearance was linked with colostrum use.

Eleven-year-old Timko is extremely pleased with colostrum. No one likes warts, especially if you're a child. According to Timko, "nothing would touch my warts. If they were removed, more would come back in their place. After taking colostrum, I have no more warts."

Many adults who have experienced the benefits of colostrum then go on and give it to their children. Dr. Brent Wells notes that he gave colostrum to his three-year-old daughter when she had a bacterial infection. "It cleared up in less than two days. I have never witnessed anything that worked so fast, and is so safe," he says.

Ronna, who uses colostrum for fibromyalgia and irritable bowel syndrome, was so pleased with the results she got that she began to give one capsule of colostrum (mixed in the child's applesauce) to her daughter every day. "She was constantly having a stuffy or runny nose," says Ronna. "Now she rarely does, except when I forget to give her the colostrum a few days in a row."

Colostrum: What Is It Good For?

Although colostrum has been around for a very long time, it has not been readily available as a supplement to the general public until recently. Therefore, we will probably be adding to the list of diseases, conditions, or symptoms for which colostrum is effective as a preventive or treatment. Only time will tell.

Colostrum can benefit more than sixty immune and autoimmune diseases, including the following: AIDS, allergies, arthritis, asthma, bronchitis, bursitis, candida, common cold, colitis, chronic fatigue syndrome, Crohn's disease, diabetes, diarrhea, fatigue, fibromyalgia, gingivitis, heart conditions, hemorrhaging, high cholesterol, irritable bowel syndrome, inflammatory bowel disease, multiple sclerosis, parasites, sinusitis, scleroderma and warts.

We have tried to answer many questions about bovine colostrum in the previous pages. But people are so interested and curious about bovine colostrum that new questions come up all the time. Without repeating what's been discussed already, here are some of the questions people are asking about this new supplement.

Can I get raw colostrum from my local dairy farmer?

Yes, your local dairy farmer can supply you with colostrum. Be sure, however, that it is fresh and has been refrigerated and not frozen. Colostrum that comes from pasture-fed cows (preferably fed organically grown grass) and cows that have not been treated with hormones, steroids, or antibiotics is the preferred source. If the colostrum is coming from just one cow, it will lack a broad base of immune factors, which is available from processed colostrum supplements.

Does colostrum interact with other supplements or prescription medications?

Colostrum does not cause any interactions with drugs, supplements, or food. It does, however, improve the assimilation and utilization of your food, supplements, and any medications you may be taking. This means you may need to change how you dose with your medications and supplements. (Note: Do not stop or change dosing of any prescription drugs you are taking without first consulting with your physician.)

Is colostrum safe if I'm pregnant or nursing?

Although colostrum has not caused any known problems in women who are pregnant or nursing, it is recommended that you consult with your physician before you taking colostrum or any drug, herb, or nutritional supplements.

Is colostrum safe for pets?

Because bovine colostrum is not species specific, it can be given to your pets without any problem. Sprinkle a little powder into their food (one-half to one teaspoon, depending on the size of the animal) and encourage them to drink plenty of water.

I've heard colostrum is good for wound healing. How can I treat such injuries?

Mix colostrum powder with sterile water or a saline solution to form a paste. Apply the paste to the affected area and cover it with a gauze bandage if necessary. Colostrum can be applied several times a day until healing has occurred.

Colostrum has many features that make it an excellent treatment for cuts, burns, surgical incisions, and abrasions. Its epithelial growth factors stimulate healing; its antibacterial and antiviral properties prevent and eliminate infection; and its anti-inflammatory abilities reduce swelling and pain

Can colostrum help my gingivitis?

Colostrum can both prevent and treat gingivitis. Make a paste as described above. Apply the paste to your gums every night before you go to bed until the gingivitis clears.

REFERENCES

1. U. Hadom, et al. Delaying colostrum intake by one day has important effects on metabolic traits and on gastrointestinal and metabolic hormones in neonatal calves. Journal of Nutrition 127 (10) (Oct. 1997): 2011-2023.

2. Paula .D. Scariati et al. A longitudinal analysis of infant morbidity and the extent of breast-feeding in the United States. Pediatrics 99(6): June 1997, p. 5.

3. Linda C. Duff, et al. Exclusive breastfeeding protects against bacterial colonization and day care exposure to otitis media. Pediatrics 100(4) (October 1997): 7.

4. PG Goyco and RC Becekman. Sudden infant death syndrome. Curr Prob Pediatr 20: 1990, 299-346.

5. Y Chen et al. Artificial feeding and hospitalization in the first 18 months of life. Pediatrics 81(1988): 58-62; Allan S. Cunningham, Breastfeeding, bottle-feeding and illness: An annotated bibliography 1986. Lactation Resource Center Nursing Mother's Association of Australia.

6. Healthy People 2000: National Health Promotion and Disease Prevention Objectives. Washington, DC: Government Printing Office; 1990:379-380. US Dept Health and Human Services pub PHS 91-50212.

7. AS Ryan. The resurgence of breastfeeding in the United States. Pediatrics 99(4): 1997. www.pediatrics.org/cgi/content/full/99/4/el2

8. Richard J. Schanler, Karen G. O'Connor, and Ruth A Lawrence. Pediatricians' practices and attitudes regarding breastfeeding promotion. Pediatrics 103(3): March 1999, 35.

9. Work Group on Breastfeeding. Breastfeeding and the use of human milk. Pediatrics 100(6) (December 1977): 103-1039.

10. ML Gwinn. Pregnancy, breastfeeding and oral contraceptives and the risk of epithelial ovarian cancer. J Clin Epidemiol 43 (1990): 559-568; MM Hreschyshyn, et al. Associations of parity, breast-feeding and birth control pills with lumbar spine and femoral neck bone densities, Am J Obstet Gynecol 159: 1988, 318-322; HJ Kalwart and BL Specker, Bone mineral loss during lactation and recovery after weaning, Obstet Gynecol 86 (1995): 26-32.

11. A Lucas, et al. Lancet February 1, 1992; CI Lanting, et al, Lancet November 12, 1994.

12. Nikki Lee, RN, MSN. Benefits of breastfeeding and their economic impact: A Report, August 1977.

13. ET Swarbrick, et al. The Immunology of Infant Feeding, New York: Plenum Press, 1980, pp. 13-20.

14. Albert B Sabin. Antipoliomylitic substance in milk from human beings and certain cows. Journal of Diseases in Children 80 (1950): 866; and Sabin, Antipoliomylitic activity of human and bovine colustrum and milk. Pediatrics 29 (1962): 105-115.

15. GP Davidson, et al. Passive immunization of children with bovine colostrum containing antibodies to human rotarirus. Lancet 2:709-712, 1989.

16. AK Mitra, et al. Hyperimmune cow colostrum reduces diarrhea due to rotavirus: a double-blind study, controlled clinical trial. Acta Paediatr 84:996-1001, 1995; BL Ungar, et al. Cessation of Cryptosporidium-associated diarrhea in an acquired immunodeficiency syndrome patient after treatment with hyperimmune bovine colostrum. Gastroenterology 98(2):486-489, Feb.1990; J Nord, et al. Treatment with bovine hyperimmune colostrum of cryptosporidial diarrhea in AIDS patients. AIDS 4(6) (June 1990):581-584, AK Bogstedt, et al. Passive immunity against diarrhea. Acta Paediatr 8:125-128, 1996.

17. Work Group of Breastfeeding, op cit.

18. Watson, et al. Journal of Dairy Research 59(3) (August 1992): 369-80.

19. CE Bruce, Natural History February 1969.

20. US News & World Report May 10, 1999; 52.

21. Ibid.

22. Ibid.

23. American Cancer Society. Cancer Facts and Figures—1997.

24. NHANES (National Health and Nutritional Examination Survey) 1988-1994. A publication of the Dept. of Health & Human Services, National Center for Health Statistics. Available through National Technical Information Service; 703-605-6000.

25. National Resource Defense Council.

26. US Department of Agriculture, Food Safety & Inspection Service news release, March 9, 1999.

27. JK Kiecolt-Glaser and R. Glaser. Stress and the immune system: Human studies. In Tasman A and Riba, MB (eds). Annual Review of Psychiatry, 11 (1991): 169-180; and S. Cohen and GM Williamson. "Stress and infectious disease in humans." Psychological Bulletin, 109 (1991): 5-24.

28. Ritchie J. Update on the management of intestinal cryptosporidiosis in AIDS. Ann Pharmacother 28 (1994): 767-778; Rump JA, et al. Treatment of diarrhea in human immunodeficiency virus-infected patients with immunoglobulins from bovine colostrum. Clin Investi 70 (1994): 588-594; Ungar BLP, et al. Cessation of Cryptosporidium-associated diarrhea in AIDS patient after treatment with hyperimmune-bovine colostrum. Gastroenterology 98 (1990): 486-489.

29. Tokuyama and Tokuyama, Cellular Biology Report 13 (United Kingdom: Harwood Academic Publishers, 1989). 251-258; Tokuyama and Tokuyama, Journal Dairy Research 60 (1993): 99-109; "Quiet Strides in the War On Cancer," Business Week 6 February 1995.

30. "First Federal Obesity Clinical Guidelines Released," National Institutes of Health Press Release, 17 June 1998. NHLBI Information Center, PO Box 30105, Bethesda MD 20824.

31. Morton Walker. Bovine colostrum offers broad-spectrum benefits for wide-ranging ailments, Townsend Letter for Doctors & Patients (April 1999): 74-80.

32. GL Francis. Purification and partial sequence analysis of insulin-like growth factor 1 from bovine colostrum, Biochemical Journal 233(1) (1986): 207-213; and GL Francis et al, Insulin-like growth factors 1 and 2 in bovine colostrum, Biochemical Journal 251 (1988): 95-103.

33. A Mero et al. "Effect of bovine colostrum supplementation on serum IGF-1, IgG, hormones, and saliva IgA during training." Jrl Appl Physiol 83 (4) (1997): 1144-1151.

34. Schwade, Muscle & Fitness May 1992.

35. Warny M, Fatimi A, Bostwick EF, et al. Bovine immunoglobulin concentrate-clostridium difficile retains C difficile toxin neutralising activity after passage through the human stomach and small intestine. Gut 44(2) (February 1999): 212-217.

36. A Pineo, et al. Biochemical Biophysiology Acta (Amsterdam) 379 (1975): 201-206.

37. Sandholm, et al. Acta Veterinaria Scandinavica. Vol. 20 (4) (1980): 469-476.

38. RJ Playford et al. Gut 44 (5) (May 1999): 653-658.

39. G. Bauriedel, et al. Chlamydia pneumoniae in coronary plaques. Increased detection with acute coronary syndrome. Dtsch Med Wochenssch 124(13) (April 1, 1999): 37-80; FL Visseren, et al. Atherosclerosis as an infectious disease. Ned Tijdschr Geneeskdl 143(6) (Feb. 6, 1999): 291-95; J. Danesch, et al. Is Helicobacter pylori a factor in coronary atherosclerosis? J Clin Microbiol 37(5) (May 1999): 1651; DP Strachan, et al., Relation of Chlamydia pnneumoniae serology to mortality and incidence of ischaemic heart disease over 13 years in the caerphilly prospective heart disease study. Br Med J 318(7190) (April 17, 1999): 1035-39; Norma Watner, The Salt Lake Tribune June 1, 1996.

40. CO Tacket et al. "Efficacy of bovine milk immunoglobulin concentrate in preventing illness after Shigella flexner challenge." American J Trop Med Hygiene 47:276-283, 1992

41. Cancer Biotech Weekly, March 1995.

42. For example: RL Wilder, et al. Hormonal regulation of tumor necrosis factor-alpha, interleukin-12 and interleukin-10 production by activated macrophages. A disease-modifying mechanism in rheumatoid arthritis and systemic lupus erythematosus. Ann N Y Acad Sci. 876 (22 June 1999): 14-31; TW Huizinga, et al. Interleukin-10 as an explanation for pregnancy-induced flare in systemic lupus erythematosus and remission in rheumatoid arthritis. Rheumatology (Oxford) 38(6) (June 1999):496-8; FM Brennan, Interleukin 10 and arthritis. Rheumatology (Oxford) 38(4) (April 1999):293-7; A Cantagrel, et al. Interleukin-1beta, interleukin-1 receptor antagonist, interleukin-4, and interleukin-10 gene polymorphisms: relationship to occurrence and severity of rheumatoid arthritis. Arthritis Rheum 42(6) (June 1999):1093-100; CM Verhoef, et al. The immune suppressive effect of dexamethasone in

rheumatoid arthritis is accompanied by upregulation of interleukin 10 and by differential changes in interferon gamma and interleukin 4 production. Ann Rheum Dis 58(1) (January 1999):49-54.

43. A. Nitsch and FP Nitsch. The clinical use of bovine colotrum. Journal of Orthomolecular Medicine 13(2) (1998): 110-118.

44. For example: AK Stewart, et al. Adenovector-mediated gene delivery of interleukin-2 in metastatic breast cancer and melanoma: results of a phase 1 clinical trial. Gene Ther 6(3) (March 1999):350-63.; M Abdel-Wahab et al. Evaluation of cell mediated immunity in advanced pancreatic carcinoma before and after treatment with interleukin-2 (IL-2). Hepatogastroenterology. 46 Suppl 1 (May 1999): 1293-6; W Den Otter et al. Local low-dose IL-2 therapy. Hepatogastroenterology. 1999 May;46 Suppl 1:1280-6; Y Ueda et al. Clinical application of adoptive immunotherapy and IL-2 for the treatment of advanced digestive tract cancer. Hepatogastroenterology. 1999 May;46 Suppl 1:1274-9.

45. MM Bittzan, et al. Inhibition of H. pylori and H. mustelae binding to lipid receptors by bovine colostrum. J Infect Dis 177 (April 1998): 955-961; Y Handa, T Saitoh, M Kawaguchi, R Misaka. Helicobacter pylori infection and histological types of gastric cancer. Nippon Shokakibyo Gakkai Zasshi 96 (6) (June 1999): 634-643; M Stolte, A Meining, Helicobacter pylori and gastric cancer. Oncologist 3 (2) (1998): 124-128.

46. Sporn et al. Science 1983; vol. 219; 1329-31. Polypeptide transforming growth factors and epithelial growth factor isolated from bovine colostrum used for wound healing in vivo.

47. E Dohn, et al. Stimulated glucose transport. Diabetes Sept 30 1990; 1028-1032.

48. M Kurokava, et al. Effects of growth factors on an intestinal epithelial cell line: Transforming growth factor beta inhibits proliferation and stimulates differentiation. Biochemical and Biophysical Research communications 142: 775-782, 1987.

49. Taken from Morton Walker. Bovine colostrum offers broad-spectrum benefits for wide-ranging ailments, Townsend Letter for Doctors & Patients (April 1999): 74-80.

50. Telephone interview, 9 June 1999 with Dr. N-M Welch.